Public Administration in Modern Society

FOUNDATIONS OF AMERICAN GOVERNMENT AND POLITICAL SCIENCE

Joseph P. Harris, Consulting Editor

Revisions and additions have been made to keep this series up to date and to enlarge its scope, but its purpose remains the same as it was on first publication: To provide a group of relatively short treatises dealing with major aspects of government in modern society. Each volume introduces the reader to a major field of political science through a discussion of important issues, problems, processes, and forces and includes at the same time an account of American political institutions. The author of each work is a distinguished scholar who specializes in and teaches the subjects covered. Together the volumes are well adapted to serving the needs of introductory courses in American government and political science.

Since Andrew Hacker's volume covers material of an essentially timeless nature only minor corrections have been made for the new printing. The notation, second edition, identifies other volumes that have been more extensively revised. The greatest expansion of material occurred in the revision which turned The President and Congress *by Rowland Egger and Joseph P. Harris into two books separately discussing the Presidency and the Congress. The authors and the editor have agreed that for the time being revision of* Public Administration in Modern Society *should be deferred.*

ANDREW HACKER: The Study of Politics: The Western Tradition and American Origins

C. HERMAN PRITCHETT: The American Constitutional System, 2D ED.

HUGH A. BONE and AUSTIN RANNEY: Politics and Voters, 2D ED.

ROWLAND EGGER: The President of the United States

JOSEPH P. HARRIS: Congress and the Legislative Process

> (The two books listed above were revised and enlarged from materials contained in the first edition of *The President and Congress* by Rowland Egger and Joseph P. Harris.)

JOHN J. CORSON and JOSEPH P. HARRIS: Public Administration in Modern Society

CHARLES O. LERCHE, JR.: America in World Affairs, 2D ED.

CHARLES R. ADRIAN: Governing Our Fifty States and Their Communities, 2D ED.

H. FRANK WAY, JR.: Liberty in the Balance: Current Issues in Civil Liberties, 2D ED.

PUBLIC ADMINISTRATION IN MODERN SOCIETY

John J. Corson

Professor of Public and International Affairs
Princeton University and
Director, McKinsey & Company, Inc.

Joseph P. Harris

Professor of Political Science
University of California, Berkeley

McGRAW-HILL BOOK COMPANY, INC.
NEW YORK / SAN FRANCISCO /
TORONTO / LONDON

**PUBLIC ADMINISTRATION
IN MODERN SOCIETY**

*This book is set in linotype Janson. The
original specimen sheets date from about
1700 and are of Dutch origin. The chapter
openings are Century Bold Condensed and
the displayed heads are News Gothic Bold.*

7 8 9 10 — BABA — 5 4

Preface

The study of public administration is a part of the larger study of American government and political science. Public administration is the means by which policies and objectives are implemented. To understand how government is administered, public administration must be studied in the context of our governmental system. The student needs to be informed about our constitutional background and legal institutions and to have an understanding of political theory, the respective roles of the legislature and the Chief Executive, and the influence of political parties and other organized groups on government.

To understand how the administration of government develops, the student must be aware of the great changes that have taken place in our society during the last half century. These changes have enormously increased—in volume and in kind—the functions placed upon government, and have required the development of a new public administration that was undreamed of at the turn of the present century. The revolution in science and technology, rapid urbanization, the increasing involvement of this country in international affairs, and the cold war have greatly altered the tasks and responsibilities of government and of those who administer our governmental agencies.

Formerly the primary objective of the study of public administration was to make government more efficient and economical. This goal is still important. But today increased emphasis is placed on the role of public administrators in the formulation of policies and programs to cope with the pressing problems and needs of a rapidly evolving, highly industrialized, and urban society. No longer is it believed that administration can be kept separate from policy and politics. Public administrators work with and under the direction of politicians, who have an indispen-

sable role in democratic government. *How to achieve democratic control over the bureaucracy—government officials and employees—so that it faithfully and effectively carries out the policies of the elected representatives and political executives is one of the leading problems of democratic governments everywhere.*

The first part of this volume, by Joseph P. Harris, deals with the major changes in modern society which have greatly increased the role of government and public administration and with organization and administrative processes in government. The second part, by John J. Corson, deals with the administration of the Federal government, including the role of the President as Chief Executive and his staff agencies, the management of the departments and agencies, and the effects of the Federal government upon the national economy. The administration of state and local governments is treated in a companion volume by Charles R. Adrian, Governing Our Fifty States and Their Communities, *and the administration of foreign affairs is discussed by Charles O. Lerche in* America in World Affairs.

We have not attempted in this short volume to describe administrative techniques and procedures, which necessarily vary from one government and one agency to another. We have attempted instead to identify and analyze those basic aspects of public administration that are of wider application, including the programs, organization, and administration of the Federal government, about which all citizens should be informed.

John J. Corson
Joseph P. Harris

Contents

**PART I INTRODUCTION TO THE STUDY OF
PUBLIC ADMINISTRATION**

1 PUBLIC ADMINISTRATION IN MODERN SOCIETY, 1

The Growth of Governmental Functions
Population Growth and Urbanization
The Impact of Science and Technology
The Impact of the Cold War
Increasing Involvement in International Affairs
The Evolving Study of Public Administration
What is Public Administration?
A Framework for the Study of Public Administration

**2 THE ORGANIZATION AND MANAGEMENT
OF PUBLIC AGENCIES, 17**

Elements of Organization
Characteristics of Big Organizations
Two Approaches to the Study of Organization
Informal Organization
Forms of Overhead Organization
The Public Administration Model of Organization
Management of Government

3 THE PUBLIC SERVICE, 36

Government as an Employer
Distinguishing Characteristics of the Public Service
Organization for Personnel Administration
Classification and Pay
Recruitment and Selection
Training and Promotion
Employee Organizations
Veterans' Preference
Loyalty and Security
Control of the Public Service
The Future of the Public Service

**PART II THE ADMINISTRATION OF THE
FEDERAL GOVERNMENT**

**4 ADMINISTERING TRADITIONAL FEDERAL
FUNCTIONS, 52**

The President and his Staff
Administering the Executive Departments
Promotion and the Public Interest
Administration through Independent Agencies
Government in the Administration of Science
Relationship of Departments and Agencies to Congress
Presidential Leadership

5 ADMINISTERING OUR NATIONAL DEFENSES, 76

Scope and Environment
The Organizational Setting
The Administrative Process Within
Strategic Planning
Mobilizing and Training Forces
Developing Future Weapons
The Task of Military Support
Utilizing the Fighting Forces
Mobilizing the Free World
Defending the Home Front
The Need for Public Support
An Evolving Framework
The Status of Civilian Control
Special Nonprofit Corporations

6 THE FEDERAL GOVERNMENT AND THE ECONOMY, 100

Supplying the Motive Power
Controlling Money and Credit
The Lending Process
Tax and Debt Policies and the Economy
Federal Expenditures: Types and Effects
The Budgetary Process
The Legislative Role
Public Versus Private Enterprise

7 REGULATING PRIVATE ENTERPRISE, 125

The Roots of Regulation
The Evolution of Regulation
Regulation of Transportation
Regulation of Utilities
Regulation of Business Structure and Practices
Regulation of Investment
Regulation and Labor Relations
Administrative Machinery for Regulation
What Regulatory Agencies Do
Distinctiveness of Regulatory Administration
Problems of Regulatory Administration
Summary

FOR FURTHER READING, 148

INDEX, 150

PUBLIC ADMINISTRATION IN MODERN SOCIETY

Chapter 1

We live in an administrative age. The food we eat, the clothes we wear, the goods we buy, the streets and highways on which we travel, the automobiles in which we ride, and the many services we enjoy—education, medical care, entertainment, recreation, protection of our lives and property, and many others—are made possible by administration. Our high standard of living, the great accomplishments in agriculture, industry, commerce, communication, travel, medicine, education, and other fields, and the spectacular developments of the nuclear age are due to advances in administration as well as in science and technology.

This volume is concerned with one branch of administration—public administration. Approximately nine million persons—one out of every eight persons gainfully employed—are employed by government. Millions of other employees work for employers who produce goods and services for government under contract, and still millions of others are members of the armed forces. Nearly one-fourth of the national income is devoted to government. We constantly place increasing tasks upon government. How well government is able to carry out these added tasks depends, in large part, on how well it is administered.

THE GROWTH OF GOVERNMENTAL FUNCTIONS

Government performs two types of functions. It provides services for its citizens; for example, it delivers the mails, cleans the streets, and operates the schools. It regulates the activities of citizens; for example, it issues licenses to those it will permit to drive automobiles, to those it will permit to fly a plane, and to those it will permit to practice medicine. In all industrial countries throughout the world there has been a constant and substantial expansion in the number and variety of each of these two governmental functions.

Government in the United States affects the life of each individual from *before* he is born until after he dies through such services as prenatal clinics, birth certificates, maternal aid services, milk inspection, kindergartens, public schools, playgrounds, and juvenile correction. Throughout his lifetime the individual enjoys governmental services, including public hospitals, public health services, marriage licenses, employment offices, water supply, police protection, the licensing of professions and trades, the inspection of factories, minimum-wage laws, labor dispute mediation, unemployment insurance, insurance of bank deposits, public housing, community planning, public parks, and recreational services. In old age he receives government old-age insurance, a death certificate is issued at his death, and if necessary the public morgue is available to care for the body.

The increase in government functions, old and new, has been accompanied by a corresponding rise in government expenditures. Since 1890, the expenditures of state and local governments have approximately doubled every decade except during the depression of

TABLE 1 PER CAPITA GOVERNMENT EXPENDITURES, 1902 AND 1957, BY FUNCTION (IN 1957 DOLLARS)

FUNCTION	1902	1957	PERCENTAGE OF INCREASE
National defense and international affairs	$ 7.45	$268.97	3,560
Education	11.74	90.81	780
Highways	7.56	46.46	615
Public welfare	1.87	20.32	1,060
Hospitals	2.08	18.61	890
Police	2.27	9.58	420
Sanitation	2.30	8.25	360
Health	0.89	5.77	640
Fire	1.84	4.66	350

SOURCE: Computed from U.S. Census reports on government expenditures.

the thirties. The increase in all government expenditures between 1902 and 1957 is shown in Table 1, which gives total per capita government expenditures for those years.

Federal expenditures have increased from one-third of all government expenditures in 1900 to two-thirds today. The great bulk of this increase has been for national defense, international relations, and the cost of past wars, which combined accounted for 79 per cent of the 1963 Federal budget. It is significant to note that since 1940 state and local government expenditures have increased at a more rapid rate than the nondefense expenditures of the Federal government.

This rapid growth in government and in public expenditures has been due largely to the revolutionary changes in society that have placed new and enlarged functions upon government. The growth of population and its concentration in metropolitan areas, the revolution in science and technology, the necessity of defending ourselves against an undeclared enemy in a cold war, and the emergence of the United States as the leader of the free world have given rise to big government and a new public administration in the United States.

POPULATION GROWTH AND URBANIZATION

The population of the United States increased from 75 million in 1900 to 180 million in 1960. At the current rate of growth, the nation will have a population of 214 million by 1970 and 260 million by

1980.[1] The rate of growth, however, has been uneven. During the decade from 1950 to 1960, urban population increased by 30 per cent, while rural areas declined by 1 per cent. Half of the 3,072 counties lost population. During the fifties persons over sixty-five years of age and those under eighteen years increased five times as rapidly as those in the age group from eighteen to sixty-five years. The dependent age groups that require the greatest government services are thus growing at a much faster rate than the productive age groups.

Simultaneously, 80 per cent of the total increase in this country's population during the fifties took place in the 212 metropolitan areas[2] of the country. Much of this growth resulted from the movement of people from the farms and small towns into the metropolitan areas. Two-thirds of this increase occurred in the suburban areas surrounding large cities, rather than in the central cities. Eleven of the twelve largest cities lost population during the decade; only Los Angeles gained. Large numbers of middle- and upper-income families moved from the central cities to the suburbs, and their places were usually taken by low-income, ill-educated families seeking opportunity. In 1960, over 113 million people lived in metropolitan areas, as compared with 85 million persons in 1950. If the trend continues, by 1970 the metropolitan areas will grow by 25 to 30 million people, and will have over two-thirds of the total population of the country.

It is in the metropolitan areas that acute social and economic problems have placed new and increasing demands upon government. The central cities pose the problems that accompany blighted areas, slums, substandard housing, increasing crime rates and juvenile delinquency, and the economic decay of business and industrial areas. Equally pressing problems are found in the growing suburbs because of the rapid increase in population, especially in the school-age group, without adequate schools and other municipal services, and usually without adequate planning and a tax base to finance needed municipal services. The transportation of millions of men and women from homes to jobs and back is a number one problem in almost all metropolitan areas.

Those who administer the metropolitan communities—the mayors, city and county managers, and department heads—are handicapped in

[1] See U.S. Bureau of the Census, *Census of Population: 1960*, vol. I, 1961; Philip M. Hauser, *Population Perspectives*, Rutgers University Press, New Brunswick, N.J., 1960.

[2] A metropolitan area is defined by the Census Bureau as an urban area including a central city of at least 50,000 population.

coping with these and other community-wide problems because of the absence of a metropolitan government with jurisdiction over the entire area, and because of the indifference of rural-dominated state legislatures.

THE IMPACT OF SCIENCE AND TECHNOLOGY

The scientific developments during the last two decades equal those of the preceding century and are continuing at an ever-accelerating pace. Revolutionary changes have occurred in agriculture, industry, commerce, transportation, communication, and other fields, and even greater changes are in prospect. More spectacular developments have occurred in the technology of warfare, where the armament of World War II and even that of the Korean War have already become obsolete. Indeed, the explosion of science and technology during the last two decades is rapidly changing American society and placing new tasks and new responsibilities on government.[3] The total expenditures of the nation for scientific activities increased from 264 million dollars in 1938 to over 15 billion dollars in 1962, an increase of nearly sixty times.

The Federal government has long had an interest in the stimulation of scientific advance and in the utilization of science. The first assistance to science by the Federal government was the establishment of the Patent Office in 1790. In 1846, Congress chartered the Smithsonian Institution for the "increase and diffusion of knowledge among men," and in 1863, it created the National Academy of Science, which was charged with the conduct of investigations of science and art at the request of government departments. Its Bureau of Standards, Geological Survey, Department of Agriculture, Corps of Engineers, and most recently Atomic Energy Commission, Department of Defense, and National Aeronautics and Space Administration have been large "users" of science and employers of scientists.

The Federal government is currently spending over 12 billion dollars annually for science, the great bulk of which is for research and development in defense, in defense-related projects, and in space re-

---

[3] For an account of the impact of science and technology on government and public administration, see Warren Weaver, "A Great Age for Science," and Thomas J. Watson, Jr., "Technological Change," in The President's Commission on National Goals, *Goals for Americans,* Prentice-Hall, Inc., Englewood Cliffs, N.J., 1960.

search. Most of this research and development is carried on by private industry and universities under contract. But the number of scientists and engineers employed by the Federal government increased from 13,631 in 1931 to 120,990 in 1958. Similar increases occurred in other professional and technical positions. Government today also requires the services of large numbers of highly skilled administrators with imagination and flexible minds to cope with the problems and needs of a rapidly changing society.

In 1945, Dr. Vannevar Bush, wartime director of the Office of Scientific Research and Development, expressed great concern in his final report over the inadequate attention government was giving to science and the lack of any organization charged with developing a science policy. Since that time substantial progress has been made in meeting this need. The National Science Foundation was established in 1950 to foster and promote basic scientific research and to coordinate the scientific activities of the government. In 1957, a Special Assistant to the President on Science was appointed, and the Science Advisory Committee, composed of distinguished nongovernment scientists, was transferred to the White House to advise the President.

Two years later another advisory body, the Federal Council on Science, consisting of representatives of the Federal departments engaged in scientific activities, was created to advise the President on science policies. This organization, however, was not deemed adequate, and in 1962, President Kennedy, with the approval of Congress, created the Office of Science and Technology in his Executive Office, to which were transferred the functions of coordinating the scientific activities of the government and advising the President.

Science and technology have made possible rapid increases in the standard of living, and promise, if we are wise enough to put new knowledge and discoveries to constructive uses, to create a life of greater abundance. Yet, not all of the changes due to science have been of benefit to man. Indeed, the survival of modern society, if not of mankind, depends on whether man can develop rapidly enough the ability to control science and put it to constructive uses. In this effort government and public administration will play a crucial role.

THE IMPACT OF THE COLD WAR

Like a dreadful, consuming blight the cold war has greatly modified the tasks of public administration in the United States since World

War II. The impact of the cold war has been greatest upon the Federal government, but it is also felt in every community, as well as in the state capitals. The cooperation of state and local government is required in providing schools, police protection, health and welfare services, highways, and recreational and other facilities for defense workers and servicemen and their families, and even more directly in the establishment of civil defense and in administering the selective military service.

The constant danger under which the American people live, as long as the cold war persists, has forced the Federal government to build a military force of unparalleled size and diversity, dispersed throughout most of the world, to protect the interests and territory of the United States and its allies. The building and maintenance of such a military force requires a vast establishment, millions of men and women with a great variety of skills, and an annual budget of approximately fifty billion dollars—more than half the total Federal budget.

It requires not only highly trained professional military men, but men who have an understanding of procurement, scientific research, the operation of aircraft and electronics industries that supply our weapons, and the operation of one of the world's largest chains of retail stores. It requires men who are highly informed about the economic, political, and social forces in each of the countries that we count as our allies, and other men who are able to interpret to the taxpayers through all means of communication what we are doing and why. In addition, it requires administrators who have an understanding of our own governmental institutions, of civil and military relations in a democracy, and of the responsibilities of public service.

INCREASING INVOLVEMENT IN INTERNATIONAL AFFAIRS

The rapid advances in the technology of transportation and most recently space communication have brought Washington closer to Moscow, Saigon, and Leopoldville than it was to Chicago in 1900. If ever the United States was an "island unto itself," it never will be again. Since World War II the United States has become inextricably involved in the social, economic, political, and racial struggles of each section of the world. It has had—by virtue of its economic, military, and political strength—the role of leadership of the free world thrust upon it. And this role, we have learned, entails large obligations.

The conduct of foreign affairs is no longer entrusted wholly to diplomats skilled in political and economic affairs, negotiation, and linguistics. The task now involves, in addition to the traditional skills of the foreign service, men and women competent to work in the threescore countries that we aid in improving their agriculture, their schools, their public health, their welfare institutions, their electric power systems, the navigation of their rivers, the irrigation of their fields, the efficiency of the methods they use to collect taxes and keep their public accounts, and numerous other activities.

Foreign relations today are conducted not only by the greatly enlarged staff of the State Department, which acts as a coordinating agency, but in varying degrees by other executive departments. Several departments have personnel attached to our embassies abroad to assist in the conduct of foreign relations; members of staff of various departments and agencies render expert advice and assistance in foreign-aid programs. All departments must keep informed about our foreign policies and developments abroad, which have an impact upon every major governmental program.

THE EVOLVING STUDY OF PUBLIC ADMINISTRATION

As these and other developments have caused government to grow, to provide ever-increasing functions and services, and to require larger and larger budgets, the administration of government and methods to improve it and make it more efficient have attracted increasing attention. In 1906, the first bureau of "municipal research" was formed in New York City by a group of leading citizens who believed that research would be more effective than political action in elevating the standards of municipal administration. Its success in promoting efficiency and economy led taxpayers in a number of other large cities to form similar research bureaus to study local government and its administration. These research bureaus made significant contributions to the improvement of local government and administration, but their influence declined as municipal government improved and research became an accepted function of government itself.

As early as 1915–1925, a number of states instituted administrative surveys of the jungle of executive departments and agencies that had been established to perform increasing functions of state governments. These studies usually resulted in the strengthening of the governor's responsibility by the consolidation of the numerous departments, boards, and commissions into a few executive departments under the governor, and by the adoption of an executive budget. The state administrative reorganization movement has continued to the present.

One of the earliest systematic studies of Federal administration was conducted by an interdepartmental committee appointed by President Theodore Roosevelt in 1905. In 1910, President Taft secured an appropriation from Congress for the work of his Commission on Efficiency and Economy. This Commission made a notable report in 1912 in which it recommended the adoption of a national budget system, but it was not until 1921 that the Budget and Accounting Act was enacted.

Since 1930, many studies of the administration of the Federal government have been made, some by official commissions, others by government departments, private organizations, and individual scholars. Especially noteworthy was the Report of the President's Committee on Administrative Management in 1937, which recommended the strengthening of the authority of the President as Chief Executive; the establishment of an Executive Office to assist him; improvements in budgeting, planning, financial, and personnel administration; and the reorganization of the executive departments and agencies. This report eloquently summed up the generally accepted principles of public administration of the period. In 1949, the Commission on the Organization of the Executive Branch of the Government (commonly known as the First Hoover Commission) made similar recommendations, which gained wide public support, and many of which were enacted into law.

The last 50 years have been marked by an increasing professionalization of the public service. Numerous professional organizations of public administrators have been formed, such as American Municipal Association, American Society for Public Administration, Council of State Governments, American Public Welfare Associations, International City Managers' Association, and National Association of Planning Officials. These organizations stimulated the study of public administration by publishing studies and professional journals such as the *Public Administration Review*, by holding annual conferences, by serving as centers of information, and sometimes by adopting codes of professional conduct for their members.

The first two texts on public administration appeared in 1926 and

1927.[4] Both authors accepted the thesis advanced earlier by Woodrow Wilson that there are "principles" of public administration which can be discovered by research and study. Leading universities began to offer courses of instruction in public administration.

During the period before World War II, the accepted goal of public administration was efficiency. A leading authority wrote in 1937:[5]

> In the science of administration, whether public or private, the basic "good" is efficiency. The fundamental objective of the science of administration is least expenditure of manpower and materials. Efficiency is thus axiom number one in the value scale of administration.

The major administrative reforms advocated during the first half of the present century as a means of securing greater efficiency and economy in government included state administrative reorganization, the strengthening of the governor as chief executive, an executive budget, civil service, the short ballot, nonpartisan local elections, and the city manager form of government. It was widely held that public administration is concerned only with the execution of public policies, which are determined by political officers. The policy-administration dichotomy has become discredited. Today it is recognized that public administrators play a vital role in the preparation and formulation of policies and programs, and advise political executives and legislative bodies, who determine policy. Moreover, many important policy decisions are necessarily delegated to executive officers. "Public administration is policy-making," wrote a leading student of public administration. "But it is not autonomous, exclusive, or isolated policy-making. It is policy-making on a field where mighty forces contend, forces engendered in and by society."[6]

Following World War II, many of the previously accepted theories

[4] Leonard D. White, *Introduction to the Study of Public Administration*, The Macmillan Company, New York, 1926; W. F. Willoughby, *Principles of Public Administration*, The Brookings Institution, Washington, D.C., 1927.
[5] Luther Gulick, "Some Values in Public Administration," in Luther Gulick and L. Urwick, *Papers on the Science of Administration*, Institute of Public Administration, New York, 1937, p. 192.
[6] Paul Appleby, *Policy and Administration*, University of Alabama Press, University, Ala., 1949, p. 170. See also Wallace S. Sayre, "A Decade in Administrative Values," *Public Administration Review*, vol. XI, 1951, pp. 1–9.

of public administration came under attack. Dwight Waldo, a leading critic, questioned the validity of "principles" borrowed from the scientific management movement in business and urged the development of a philosophy or theory of administration based upon broader study and a recognition that public administration cannot be fruitfully studied apart from its political and social setting.[7]

Another critic, Herbert Simon, proposed the development of a new science of administration based on theories and methodology of logical positivism. The focus of such a science would be decision making. He maintained that to be scientific it must exclude value judgments and concentrate attention on facts, adopt precise definition of terms, apply rigorous analysis, and test factual statements or postulates about administration. "An administrative science, like any science, is concerned purely with factual statements. There is no place for ethical statements in the study of science."[8]/Critics of Simon objected that the exclusion of values, which are an essential part of policy determination, would limit the study of public administration to mechanical, routine, and unimportant aspects.

Another recent trend in the study of both private and public administration is the emphasis on research in human relations, motivations, incentives, and communication. The pioneering studies which resulted from the experiments in the Hawthorne plant of the Western Electric Company in the late twenties challenged many prevailing ideas about incentives and human behavior in groups. Since the war similar studies have been carried on at a number of universities. These studies of human behavior stress the human aspect of administration; the need of employees for recognition, security, and ego-satisfaction; and the importance of the social environment and group attitudes in work situations. They reach the conclusion that employee-oriented supervision is more effective than production-minded, authoritarian supervision.[9]

WHAT IS PUBLIC ADMINISTRATION?

There are various definitions of public administration. To begin with, it relates to the activities carried on by government. In a brilliant

[7] *The Administrative State*, The Ronald Press Company, New York, 1948.
[8] *Administrative Behavior*, The Macmillan Company, New York, 1947, p. 253.
[9] For recent useful studies of human relations see Rensis Likert, *New Patterns of Management*, McGraw-Hill Book Company, Inc., New York, 1961.

essay written in 1887, Woodrow Wilson defined public administration as "the detailed and systematic execution of public law."[10] More recent text writers have defined public administration as "all those operations having for their purpose the fulfillment or enforcement of public policy" and "the activities of groups cooperating to accomplish the common goals of government." Public administration is decision making, planning the work to be done, formulating objectives and goals, working with the legislature and citizen organizations to gain public support and funds for government programs, establishing and revising organization, directing and supervising employees, providing leadership, communicating and receiving communications, determining work methods and procedures, appraising performance, exercising controls, and other functions performed by government executives and supervisors. It is the action part of government, the means by which the purposes and goals of government are realized.

DISTINGUISHING CHARACTERISTICS The basic principles and processes of administration are much the same for a government bureau, a store, a factory, an office, a hospital, a church, or a university. Despite these similarities, there are important differences between public and business administration. The differences sketched here indicate some of the distinguishing characteristics of public administration.

1. The prime purpose of public administration is to serve the public; of business administration, to produce a profit for the owners of the business. This provides the business administrator with a single objective criterion to measure the performance of the enterprise and the success of each separate part, as each store in a chain-store operation. The drive for profits forces the business administrator to watch costs, to seek improvements in operations, to discharge incompetent employees, and to maintain responsibility of subordinates for results. The public administrator has no similar criterion of accomplishment of the various and often vaguely defined objectives of government activities. How is he to judge, for example, the performance of a recreation center, a prenatal clinic, or a welfare program? The great challenge of the public administrator is to formulate clearcut objectives in operational terms so that accomplishment can be accurately measured.

[10] "The Study of Administration," *Political Science Quarterly*, vol. 2, pp. 197–222, June, 1887.

2. The public administrator is responsible for the simultaneous performance of multiple functions with different and sometimes contradictory objectives. For example, the Administrator of the Federal Agency for International Development is simultaneously responsible for providing economic aid to underdeveloped countries, for distributing surplus American farm products, and for encouraging the development of democratic free enterprise in the countries he serves. He is required to steer a difficult course in the midst of anomalies, contradictions, and counterpressures from the competing publics served. The public administrator's task accordingly is more diverse, complex, and difficult than that of the business administrator. The businessman ordinarily is in charge of a single operation or related operations and is seldom subjected to the counterpressures that perplex the public official.

3. The public administrator's activities are fixed by law; he may not undertake others without legislative authority. The business executive, on the other hand, is free to select those activities that promise to be profitable, and to discontinue others which fail to show a profit. Many activities, such as building parks and playgrounds, which are deemed essential to society are undertaken by government because they cannot be carried on profitably or satisfactorily by private enterprise.

4. The discretion and freedom of action of the public administrator is markedly limited. Numerous laws, regulations, and reviews exercised by the legislature, by political executives, and by central staff agencies (e.g., the Civil Service Commission) limit his discretion and his choice of methods as to how and what he shall do. Such controls are designed to ensure that public activities are carried on in accordance with legislative and executive policies, and to prevent abuses or misuse of political power or of public funds. Although business is subject to certain governmental regulations, these regulations are not comparable to those which apply to the conduct of government activities.

5. The public administrator carries on his work in a "glass bowl." His actions are exposed to public review and criticism at all times. His mistakes tend to be widely publicized, and his achievements often pass unnoticed. He has both a problem and an obligation. As James Forrestal wrote in a letter to a friend, "The difficulty of Government work is that it not only has to be well done, but the public has to be convinced that it is being well done. In other words, there is a neces-

sity both for competence and exposition, and I hold it is extremely difficult to combine the two in the same person."[11]

6. The public administrator must maintain a high degree of consistency in his actions. He must serve the public without discrimination; if he makes an exception in applying the traffic or tax laws to one man, all are entitled to similar treatment. The business administrator is subject to no similar requirement; indeed, it may be poor business to treat the small customer and the large customer alike!

7. The public administrator works continually for, with, and under the direction of politicians—the elected representatives of the people and political executives appointed to carry out the policies of the party in power. In a representative democracy, politics plays an indispensable role, often preventing the administrator from taking actions that do not have public support. The most able public administrators are keenly aware of political factors that affect public policy and are able to work effectively with their political bosses.

AN ART OR A SCIENCE? Early writers regarded public administration as potentially a science that would emerge as the result of study and research. In the essay cited above, Woodrow Wilson referred to the "science of public administration" and urged its study "to rescue executive methods from the confusion and costliness of empirical experiment and set them on the foundations laid deep in principle." Charles A. Beard, another pioneer in the field, maintained that public administration is a body of "exact knowledge derived from experience and observation. . . . It is as much a general science as economics or psychology or biology, and more of a science than history or politics."[12]

Public administration can never become an exact science, for it relates to human behavior and the cooperative activities of individuals in groups. But if the study of governmental operations cannot yield scientific principles or laws comparable to those of the exact sciences, it has already produced concepts, theories, and a body of knowledge relating to the administrative processes that are used in government.

Formerly the study of public administration was closely identified with the study of law, since the primary task of administration is the

[11] James Forrestal, *Diaries*, edited by Walter Millis and E. S. Duffield, The Viking Press, Inc., 1951, p. 300.
[12] "Philosophy, Science and Art of Public Administration," in Dwight Waldo, *Issues and Ideals in Public Administration*, McGraw-Hill Book Company, Inc., New York, 1953, p. 77.

execution of law and its activities are circumscribed by law. As the study of public administration matured, it became concerned with ways and means of achieving efficiency and economy in the management of governmental agencies and human relations and has turned to other fields of knowledge. The study of public administration today is closely identified with political science, which is the study of government. It draws also upon the other social sciences: economics, business administration, sociology, psychology and social psychology, statistics, history, and anthropology. The public administrator needs to have a deep understanding of the world in which we live and to be able to utilize the research studies and tools of analysis of the various fields of learning.

A FRAMEWORK FOR THE STUDY OF PUBLIC ADMINISTRATION

The study of public administration includes the following major areas:

1. *The "world" of public administration:* its environment and setting, the constitutional and governmental system, public institutions and traditions, the ecology of administration. The evolving pattern of cooperative federalism in the United States, under which Federal, state, and local governments jointly participate and finance an increasing number of governmental functions is a good illustration of an institution which has had profound effects on administration.

2. *Organization:* theories and practice, "models" of organization, how government agencies are organized to perform their various and widely different functions, formal and informal organizations. For example, what form of organization is best suited for the administration of a large-scale scientific program such as atomic energy? Why was a different form chosen for the National Aeronautics and Space Administration?

3. *Administrative processes:* functions of executives; planning, decision making, coordination, direction, motivation, evaluation, and control; executive leadership. For example, how do these processes in a large government agency such as the Social Security Administration with its 35,000 employees differ from those utilized by the Pennsylvania Railroad?

4. *The public service:* distinguishing characteristics; changing personnel requirements; recruitment, selection, training, promotion, and compensation of public employees; the career system and executive development; employee relations.

5. Financial administration: budgeting, accounting, auditing, control.

6. Politics and administration: the impact of political parties and pressure groups on administration. How do government departments and agencies work with powerful organized groups, whose support and cooperation is often essential to effective administration, without losing their independence of action?

7. The control of administration: the means by which the bureaucracy—the great body of government officials and employees—is made responsible and responsive to the elected representatives of the people and to the public. For example, by what means are the uniformed military services controlled and directed in their activities by the civilian heads of these agencies, the President, and the Congress?

These subject areas provide a framework for the study of public administration, and should be kept in mind by the student in considering the administrative organization processes described and analyzed in the following chapters.

Review Questions

1. Why have government functions increased in modern society? What activities have increased most?

2. What effects has the growth of population had on public administration?

3. Discuss the impact the cold war has had on public administration.

4. How is the job of the public administrator affected by the explosion of science and technology? Forecast future changes due to scientific developments.

5. Trace the significant trends and movements in the study of public administration.

6. Why is the study of public administration important in modern society? How does public administration differ from business administration?

7. What are the major areas of knowledge that are included in the study of public administration?

8. Discuss the various controls of public administration in a democratic government.

THE ORGANIZATION AND MANAGEMENT OF PUBLIC AGENCIES

Chapter 2

Two fundamental questions concern the top officials of any organization —in government, in business, or in other forms of enterprise. First, what shall the organization do? Second, how can it be accomplished with the maximum efficiency and at the minimum cost? Public administrators—the managers of public agencies and their assistants—play a role in both types of decisions. That role involves advising the political heads of state and the legislature on new policies and programs to cope with changing needs and problems, and formulating plans to carry out these policies. Finally, it includes responsibility for a major part in the direction or management of the agency, whether it be a municipal police department or the U.S. Employment Service.

James Reston, the noted correspondent of *The New York Times*, wrote early in 1962 that the ability of this country as a nation to adjust to the rapid changes in society "is vital to its own security and to the security of the free world." Public administrators, particularly those in positions of leadership in the Federal government, must lead in making such needed adjustments as, for example, modification of long-standing, deeply entrenched tariff policies to adapt to the development of the European Common Market. To cope with the problems of the rapidly changing world of today, public administrators must have not only skill in management but also a deep understanding of our political institutions; an awareness of changing economic, social, and technological trends; imagination; and flexibility of mind.

This chapter introduces the student of public administration to two major aspects of the job of running a public agency: organization and management. These subjects are closely related. They are treated separately here for convenience of analysis, but in practice they are inseparable. Logically, organization precedes management, for an activity must be organized before it is managed. But in practice the continual modification of organization and the management of the people and processes go hand in hand.

ELEMENTS OF ORGANIZATION

In the organization of a baseball team, a grocery store, a government bureau or department, or an insurance company, there are five elements: objectives, specialization, hierarchy, coordination, and authority. An organization may be defined as a group of persons who cooperate in the accomplishment of *objectives* upon which they are agreed. The performance of the group will be influenced by how well the objectives are understood and supported by its members. Objectives change with changing problems and needs and must be restated and redefined from time to time. Government departments almost always have numerous objectives, usually competing with one another and at times conflicting. This is why the job of the public administrator, who must steer a course amid anomalies and inconsistencies, is usually more difficult than that of the private administrator.

An organization distributes work so that workers may *specialize*. In the comic strip "Peanuts," Charlie Brown, captain of the baseball team, declared: "I'll tell you what I'm going to do; I'm going to write down on this sheet of paper, each fellow's name, the position he plays and what he is expected to do, and if that isn't organization, I don't know what organization is." The assignment of specialized tasks to each member of an enterprise is an element—but it is not the whole—of organization.

An organization provides for *coordination*. The efforts of workers specializing in various tasks must be effectively interrelated. This is accomplished by defining each worker's job, and by grouping workers doing related tasks under the same boss, and groups of workers performing related tasks similarly under a common boss. For each boss the "span of control," that is, the number of individuals he is expected to direct, must be limited if he is to achieve coordination.

An organization is built about a *hierarchy*. There must be clearly established channels of command, communication, and control. Workers and supervisors must clearly understand from whom they take orders and to whom they report. The vertical lines of responsibility within an organization must be defined and kept clear.

An organization fixes *authority*. Charlie Brown might have pursued his analysis of organization by declaring who would call the plays of the team, for when men work together (or play together) someone must have authority to give direction, to resolve differences among individuals working on related tasks.

In more formal terms, a leading authority has defined organization as "a system of consciously coordinated activities or forces of two or more persons."[1] Another author has defined it as the "arrangement of personnel for facilitating the accomplishment of some agreed purpose through the allocation of functions and responsibilities."[2] Organization provides the means whereby the efforts of large numbers of employees are directed and coordinated.

CHARACTERISTICS OF BIG ORGANIZATIONS

The characteristics of big organizations differ markedly from those of small organizations, in which face-to-face contacts between the

---

[1] Chester I. Barnard, *The Functions of the Executive*, Harvard University Press, Cambridge, Mass., 1938, p. 73.
[2] John M. Gaus, "A Theory of Organization in Public Administration," in *The Frontiers of Administration*, The University of Chicago Press, Chicago, 1936, p. 66.

leaders and the rank and file of employees are the rule rather than the exception. Planning, coordination, and control are relatively simple in a small organization, but highly complex in a big organization, requiring an elaborate organizational structure. The rise of big organizations in business and government has been one of the most significant developments in modern society. Though bigness is often deplored because of its tendency to reduce the individual employees to the status of a cog in the vast machine, the economies of large-scale operations have led inexorably to the growth of big organizations.

Although big organizations produce different products and render different kinds of services, they have similar characteristics and tend to operate in a similar manner. All arrange skills and relationships in order to perform the activities necessary to achieve their goals and to secure continuity and stability. All develop standardized methods and procedures. In all organizations there is competition and conflict between authority based upon position and authority based upon expertness. And most big organizations have the characteristics of specialization, hierarchy, status, oligarchy, rationality, and the search for efficiency.[3]

One of the earliest systematic analyses of the characteristics of big organizations or "bureaucracy" (the words are used here synonymously) was made by the German sociologist Max Weber early in the present century. Weber did not use the term "bureaucracy" in a derogatory sense, as it is commonly used today, but as a term descriptive of all big organizations, public and private. He regarded bureaucratic organization as far superior to other forms of organization that had preceded it, and in fact, as essential to the modern state and corporation. "The decisive reason for the advance of bureaucratic organization," he wrote, "has always been its purely technical superiority over any other form of organization."[4]

Weber found the following common characteristics of bureaucratic organizations:

1. The authority and jurisdiction of officials are prescribed, regulated, and controlled by a set of rules, laws, and administrative regulations.

[3] See Robert Presthus, *The Organizational Society*, Alfred A. Knopf, Inc., New York, 1962, especially chaps. 1 and 2.
[4] Max Weber, "Bureaucracy" (translated by Hans Gerth and C. Wright Mills), *From Max Weber*, Oxford University Press, Fair Lawn, N.J., 1946, p. 214.

2. Administration is carried on by full-time employees who are selected for their qualifications, especially trained in their duties, and given a status with permanence of tenure and pensions.

3. Offices are arranged in a hierarchy of levels of graded authority in an ordered system of super- and subordination in which the lower offices are supervised by higher ones.

4. Administration is based upon written records that are preserved; the body of officials and these records and files make up the "bureau" or "office."

5. Administration is conducted under general rules, which are more or less stable and comprehensive.

Weber's pioneering essay had a great impact on subsequent sociological studies of organization, but was only a beginning of the systematic study of bureaucratic organizations. He gave little or no attention to the individual in the organization, a subject which has been the focus of most sociological studies of organization in recent years. The extensive use of rules and regulations to control every act of the official, which Weber looked upon with favor, is widely criticized today as inimical to effective and efficient administration. Weber overlooked the importance of goals in organization, and evidently was unaware of the struggle between authority based upon rank and position and authority as a function of expertness. Although his findings have been modified and supplemented by subsequent studies, his essay is recognized as a classic description of bureaucratic organization.

TWO APPROACHES TO THE STUDY OF ORGANIZATION

The importance of organization in modern society is attested by the many recent studies and publications on the theory and characteristics of organization and human behavior in organizations.[5] Two distinct

---

[5] See Chris Argyris, *Personality and Organization,* Harper & Row, Publishers, Incorporated, New York, 1957; Amatai Etzioni (ed.), *Complex Organization: A Sociological Reader,* Holt, Rinehart and Winston, Inc., New York, 1961; Mason Haire (ed.), *Modern Organization,* John Wiley & Sons, Inc., New York, 1961; Rensis Likert, *New Patterns of Management,* McGraw-Hill Book Company, Inc., New York, 1961; Victor A. Thompson, *Modern Organization,* Alfred A. Knopf, Inc., New York, 1961; Sidney Mailick and Edward H. Van Ness (eds.), *Administration Behavior,* Prentice-Hall, Inc., Englewood Cliffs, N.J., 1962; James G. March and Herbert A. Simon, *Organizations,* Graduate School of Industrial Administration, Carnegie Press, Carnegie Institute of Technology, Pittsburgh, Pa., 1958; John M. Pfiffner and Frank G.

approaches are used in these studies. The first and older approach followed by students of administration deals primarily with the structure of organization, allocation of functions and authority, specialization, coordination, overhead direction and control, span of control, the role of "line" and "staff" units, government corporations, and relations of the central headquarters to field offices. The second approach is that of sociologists and social psychologists, whose primary attention is devoted to the individual and human behavior in organization. Students of administration have focused attention on the official or formal structure of organization, while behaviorists have inquired into individual and group behaviors, and the role of unofficial, or "informal," organizations.

Clearly both approaches are essential to an understanding of organization and the motivation of individuals within an organization. The older studies of organization, which were based largely upon observation rather than empirical research, failed to give adequate attention to the individual employee and his needs. The behavioral studies of organization, on the other hand, usually give little or no attention to the formal structure, which is regarded as of little importance. Students of administration have stressed the importance of overhead planning, direction, and control, of authority commensurate with responsibility, of clearcut assignment of duties and responsibilities, and the need for adequate supervision throughout an organization. Behavioral studies of organization indicate, however, that authoritarian supervision and too much emphasis upon authority, controls, and the administrative hierarchy tends to depress employee motivation and result in low levels of performance, and that employee-oriented supervision is conducive to high motivation and levels of production.

Despite these differences in approach, there is in fact little necessary conflict between the findings of the older studies of the formal structure of organization and the more recent studies of behavior. The kind of supervision suggested by recent behavioral studies may be adopted by widely different types of organizations. Studies of human behavior in organizations, dating from the Hawthorne plant studies in the late 1920s, have had a profound influence upon supervisory practices in government and business.

Sherwood, *Administrative Organization*, Prentice-Hall, Inc., Englewood Cliffs, N.J., 1960; Robert Presthus, *The Organizational Society*, Alfred A. Knopf, Inc., New York, 1962; Philip Selznick, *Leadership in Administration*, Harper & Row, Publishers, Incorporated, 1957.

INFORMAL ORGANIZATION

The organization of any large body of men is highly complex; it is seldom accurately portrayed by organization charts, for boxes and lines on a piece of paper cannot describe the myriad of relationships and the actual power structure. Every administrative organization is also a social organization, consisting of persons in different occupational groups and status levels, each interacting with others in accordance with well-established patterns which are generally accepted. "Most of the individuals who live among these patterns come to accept them as obvious and necessary truths and to react as they dictate. Both the kind of behavior that is expected of a person and the kind of behavior that he can expect of others are prescribed by these patterns."[6]

In addition to the official or formal organization, there are informal organizations based not upon official authority, but upon personal and group ties.[7] The informal organizations may take a wide variety of forms. They may assist the formal organization in the accomplishment of the official objectives, or they may advance interests and objectives that run counter to those of the formal organization. The heads of many organizations use a "kitchen cabinet" of persons in whom they have confidence and to whom they turn for information, advice, and assistance. These persons may hold no official position in the formal organization yet exert great power.

Informal groups arise in a variety of ways. They are usually based upon personal relationships, and are often bolstered by professional status, class, racial, religious, or other ties. Informal organizations seek to advance the real or imaginary interests of the group and its leaders, which usually vary from those of the official organization, and at times will be directly opposed. It is well to recognize that informal organizations exist in all formal organizations and are not necessarily harmful, but may facilitate teamwork and collaboration.

FORMS OF OVERHEAD ORGANIZATION

The overhead organization of government departments and agencies usually takes one of the following forms: (1) a single head, who is usually appointed by the chief executive, but in some instances is

[6] F. J. Roethlisberger and William J. Dickson, *Management and the Worker,* Harvard University Press, Cambridge, Mass., 1939, p. 554.
[7] See Chester Barnard, *The Functions of the Executive,* Harvard University Press, Cambridge, Mass., 1938, chap. IX.

elected by the voters or appointed by the legislative body; (2) boards or commissions (the terms are generally used interchangeably) consisting of three or more members, who are normally appointed by the chief executive for fixed terms of office; and (3) government corporations headed by a board of directors and an executive officer appointed by the board.

The single-headed department is most widely used. A single head is invariably used for bureaus and other subordinate units within departments and agencies. This form of organization provides unity of command and definite responsibility for administration, and facilitates prompt decisions, effective leadership, and vigorous administration. The position of head of a large department or bureau is one of great prestige, power, and responsibility, and ordinarily attracts persons of high qualifications, which is not always true of commissions.

Commissions are used principally for activities requiring careful deliberation and the judgment of several minds, whereas a single head is used for activities that are largely administrative. Commissions are often used for quasi-legislative and quasi-judicial functions, such as the regulation of industry, commerce, and the professions, but it should be noted that regulatory activities are also assigned to regular executive departments. The "independent regulatory commissions" of the Federal government, such as the Interstate Commerce Commission, the Federal Communications Commission, the Securities and Exchange Commission, and others are given considerable independence from the President because their members are appointed for relatively long, fixed terms of office, usually with overlapping terms.

Commissions are often utilized for new programs involving the development of important policies which the legislature is reluctant to entrust to a single administrator. The Federal Social Security program, for example, was initially assigned to a board, but after the program was well established, the board was abolished and a single commissioner was placed in charge. The Atomic Energy Commission was created to administer this new program of such great importance to the country that Congress was unwilling to assign it to a single head. On the other hand, a single administrator was placed in charge of the National Aeronautics and Space Administration because it was recognized that vigorous leadership would be required.

Commissions are often used in state and local governments for administrative activities, usually with unfortunate results, for a multiple-headed body is not suitable for administration. It is not uncommon for a combination of a commission and an executive officer to be used, the commission being assigned the function of deciding upon policies, and the executive officer charged with administration. The arrangement seldom works well, for there is no clearcut line between policy and administration, and commissions are prone to meddle in administrative matters. Commissions are often used for activities where the representation of particular groups in the population is deemed essential. Election administration, for example, is often entrusted to bipartisan boards, and boards of health are usually drawn largely from the medical profession. Commissions may also be used as a device to gain public support for an activity, as, for example, parks and recreation. Citizen boards usually become the leading advocates of activities which they administer.

Government corporations are used widely by governments throughout the world for the conduct of activities that are primarily commercial. President Truman stated in his 1948 budget message that "experience indicates that the corporate form of organization is peculiarly adapted to the administration of government programs which are predominantly of a commercial character—those which are revenue producing and are at least potentially self-sustaining, and involve a large number of businesslike transactions with the public." Government has found it necessary to engage in business enterprises to provide essential services that cannot be economically or satisfactorily provided by private initiative.

In 1952, the Federal government was the sole owner of 39 corporations and in addition owned part of the stock of 24 mixed-ownership corporations. The large majority of these were engaged in extending credit to farmers, homeowners, businessmen, foreign governments, and others. Government corporations were also operating power and synthetic rubber plants, tin smelters, railways, canals, hotels, steamship and barge lines, terminals and harbor facilities, distributing electric power, insuring crops, and conducting other activities.[8] The Tennessee Valley Authority is one of the world's largest generators of electric power, while the Commodity Credit Corporation in the United States Department of Agriculture purchases, stores, sells, and advances loans to farmers on basic agricultural crops in the support of agricultural prices. The St. Lawrence Seaway Corporation was cre-

[8] Harold Seidman, "The Theory of the Autonomous Government Corporation: A Critical Appraisal," *Public Administration Review*, vol. 12, pp. 89–96, 1952.

ated to construct and operate great public works in connection with the opening of the St. Lawrence River and the Great Lakes to ocean-going vessels.

Government corporations and authorities are used widely by state and local governments to operate ports, bridges, toll roads, and to provide water, electricity, and other local services. It should be noted, however, that most municipally owned public utilities, such as water, transportation, and electricity, are operated as regular city departments.

Government corporations ordinarily operate from their own revenues, keep their own accounts, may sue and be sued as a business corporation, and are free of many of the regulations and controls that apply to executive departments and agencies. They are able to act quickly, take business risks, and manage their affairs with the flexibility and initiative of a business enterprise.

Government corporations, however, are not free from control by the government. Federal corporations must be chartered by Congress and the officers in charge are usually appointed by the President with the approval of the Senate. They are required to submit annual budgets to the President for review and submission to Congress for its information. If public funds are appropriated for the use of corporations, they are subject to the same type of review as the budgets for other activities. The accounts of Federal corporations are audited by the Comptroller General, who is directed by law to conduct a "business type" of audit and report his findings to Congress for its consideration.

THE PUBLIC ADMINISTRATION MODEL OF ORGANIZATION

The following "model" consists of a group of concepts, ideas, or "principles" of organization widely held by writers and public administrators. These concepts, however, are not universally followed, for practice usually falls short of theory. They should not be regarded as immutable principles or laws governing organization, but rather as hypotheses or criteria for diagnosing organizational problems.

1. The executive organization of governments should be *integrated*, that is, the heads of executive departments and agencies should be appointed by and responsible to the chief executive, and in turn they should appoint and direct the activities of their subordinates. The organization is thus in the form of an administrative *hierarchy* in which the line of authority extends from the chief executive through subordinate officials to the rank and file of employees.

The integrative principle was stated by the First Hoover Commission in 1949 as one of its major recommendations.[9]

> Under the President, the heads of departments must hold full responsibility for their departments. There must be a clear line of authority reaching down through every step of the organization and no subordinate should have authority independent from that of his superior.

The integrative principle is firmly established in the Federal government by the Constitution, which vests the executive power in the President, who appoints the heads of all executive departments and agencies, by and with the advice and consent of the Senate, and has the sole power of removal. In the states and in local governments, however, it is often violated by the popular election of the heads of certain executive departments, and, indeed, there is no chief executive officer in most county governments.

2. Government activities should be assigned to a relatively small number of executive departments, each conducting a major function of government or a group of related functions, such as those relating to defense, agriculture, public health, welfare, public works, or conservation. It is desirable that the number of departments be limited so that the number of department heads reporting to the chief executive will not place an undue burden upon him.

3. Each executive department and agency should be organized into bureaus and other subordinate units, to which are assigned definite duties and responsibilities, preferably of a homogeneous character. Every necessary activity should be assigned to a specific unit or official so that there will be definite responsibility for its proper performance.

4. Activities may be assigned to governmental units on the basis of (*a*) purpose or function, (*b*) process, (*c*) clientele, (*d*) geography, or a combination of these. Executive departments are usually assigned a major function or a group of related functions, as, for example, public health, welfare, agriculture, police, etc. Subordinate units are often assigned a particular operation or process, as the keeping of accounts or the operation of certain machines. Organization by process

---

[9] The Commission on the Organization of the Executive Branch of the Government, *General Management of the Executive Branch*, Washington, 1949, p. 34.

facilitates specialization and the economical use of skilled personnel and expensive machines. Organization by clientele, as the Indian Service and the Veterans Administration, is used when the government provides special services for a group of the population, which cannot be administered satisfactorily by the regular executive departments. Departments or bureaus that serve a large area organize geographically by establishing regional or field offices to serve the public.

5. Unnecessary duplication and overlapping of functions and activities should be avoided because they are wasteful of manpower and prevent effective planning. Some duplication, however, is unavoidable. Numerous Federal agencies, for example, administer hospitals, including the Public Health Service, the Army, Navy, and Air Force, Indian Service, Veterans Administration, and others. It would not be practicable for all government hospitals to be administered by a single department. Certain activities, such as budgeting, accounting, personnel administration, and maintaining records and files, are carried on by all departments and units as a part of their operations, and should not be regarded as duplication. In some situations duplication may be utilized to speed operations or to provide competition.

6. The assignment of functions, authority, and responsibilities to organizational units and to individual employees should be definite, clearcut, and understood; authority should be commensurate with responsibility. Without adequate authority and the means to perform the assigned tasks, the head of a unit cannot be held responsible for results. Vague and uncertain assignments result in confusion, unnecessary conflicts, and the frustration of employees, though the assignment of duties should not be so rigid as to discourage initiative.

7. The principle of unity of command requires that each employee, including supervisors, take orders from and be supervised by one and only one supervisor. Technical specialists may be used to instruct employees in their duties, however, without violating the rule of unity of command, provided it is clearly understood that orders are given only by the supervisor.

8. The number of persons reporting to a supervisor should not be more than he can effectively supervise. The "span of control" of the supervisor should not exceed his span of attention. There is no agreed number of employees who may be supervised by a supervisor, or of administrative units that may be directed by an executive. Much depends on the nature of the work performed, the kind and degree of supervision required, whether the work is performed under the imme-

diate eye of the supervisor, and the competence and abilities of the supervisor and the employees.

9. Decisions should be delegated whenever practicable to the officers in charge of operations in order that they may be made by persons who have the greatest information. Delegation of authority avoids bottlenecks, facilitates prompt action, increases employee morale, and establishes definite responsibility for results. Centralization of policy, however, must precede decentralization of administration. Regional and field offices cannot perform their functions effectively unless they have well-defined policies and objectives to guide them, and are provided with funds, trained personnel, and the means with which to carry on their assigned duties.

10. Staff units should be used to serve, assist, and advise operating or line units, but not to give orders. Staff units are of various types, including housekeeping (maintenance of buildings, central files, car pools), administrative services (personnel administration, payrolls, accounting, purchasing, supply), control (planning, budgeting, legal), and technical (standards of performance, scientific, etc.).

CRITICISMS   The above model has been criticized for its undue stress upon the formal aspects of organization to the neglect of individual and group behaviors in organizations and the role of informal or unofficial organizations. One writer has contended that certain of the alleged principles are little more than contradictory proverbs.[10]

Other writers maintain that some of the accepted principles of organization are inconsistent with the demands of mature individuals for ego-satisfaction and require them to act in a submissive, dependent, and immature manner.[11] In studies of organization, increasing attention is given to human relations and individual and group behaviors, which affect the formal structure of organization. Undue emphasis upon authority, hierarchy, supervision, and control may act as a depressant upon employee motivation and self-realization.

MANAGEMENT OF GOVERNMENT

Organization provides the structure for the conduct of the work of a government; management provides the leadership, planning, direc-

[10] Herbert Simon, *Administrative Behavior*, The Macmillan Company, New York, 1947.
[11] See Chris Argyris, "The Individual and Organization: Some Problems of Adjustment," *Administrative Science Quarterly*, vol. 2, pp. 1–24, June, 1957.

tion, and control. The importance of management in business and industry is widely recognized, but the need for able management in government is often overlooked.

Government executives may be divided into two classes: political executives and career executives. In the Federal government political executives are appointed by the President, usually from outside the civil service. They are the secretaries of departments, heads of agencies, the undersecretaries and assistant secretaries, and perhaps a thousand other lesser officials. In a democratic government it is essential that the chief executive be permitted to select the heads of the executive departments and agencies and other top officials who are responsible to him for the administration of the departments, advise him on policies, and speak for his administration before the legislative body and the public. Without the aid of political executives of his own choosing, the elected chief executive would be unable to control the activities of the departments and carry out the policies and programs upon which he has been elected.

Formerly political executives were commonly drawn from public life and were usually chosen for political reasons. Today they are frequently drawn from business, industry, education, and the professions and are chosen ordinarily for their executive and professional qualifications. Political executives are not necessarily politicians, but must be able to work effectively with political leaders.

The career executives, who are chosen from the civil service, direct the operations of the government; many serve as assistants and advisers to the political executives. They head many, but not all, of the major bureaus and almost all of the staff offices and other organizational units. They fill the thousands of intermediate and lower-level managerial and staff positions, including heads of regional and field offices. Through extensive experience in government administration they have government know-how. Many are professionally trained in the activities they direct; some are trained in public administration; others have acquired administrative expertise by long experience. Government today has great need for able and highly trained career executives to manage its large and complex programs and to assist political executives in formulating programs and policies.

TASKS OF MANAGEMENT The management of government departments and agencies, irrespective of the programs and activities which they administer, involves the performance of certain basic functions. This does not mean, however, that all executives perform the same functions. Political executives usually devote most of their attention to policies and external relations, while career executives, as a rule, are primarily concerned with operations. The job of the executive who heads an old and well-established agency differs greatly from that of the head of a new agency, who must build the organization and develop policies and public support. The management of a scientific agency is quite different from that of other agencies. Some executive positions call for innovation, while others require stability; some involve primarily public relations while others are concerned largely with internal operations.

Despite the differences in their roles, executives perform the following tasks, or see to it that they are performed by others.

1. Define and clarify objectives. Broad objectives of government departments are specified in legislation, but within the framework of law, higher executives spend much of their time in defining objectives, making them more explicit and operational, and in communicating them to subordinates. The general objective assigned to a department is usually clear (e.g., a police department protects life and property and preserves law and order), but it needs to be restated and elaborated in terms of specific goals (e.g., reduction of the juvenile crime rate) in order to serve as a guide to administration. Carefully considered objectives give purpose and meaning to activities, enhance employee morale, and facilitate coordination and cooperation throughout an agency.

2. Advise the legislature on policies and programs. A large part of the legislation relating to government activities today originates in the departments concerned. This is due to the increasing complexity and technical character of government activities. The legislative body looks to the departments to recommend needed legislation and to give technical and policy advice concerning pending legislation.

3. Plan work programs. Government activities are carried out through work programs, which include (1) plans of the activities to be undertaken; (2) estimates of the personnel, equipment, materials, and funds that will be required; (3) decisions concerning the work procedures and methods to be used; and (4) time schedules. The Forest Service, for example, prepares annual work programs for fire protection, reforestation, recreation, and numerous other activities.

4. Plan and maintain the organization. Organizations are dynamic and need to be revised from time to time to meet changing needs and to utilize improved techniques. Executives devote much of their attention to revising the organization and reassigning personnel in order to increase efficiency and to carry out new policies and programs.

5. Staff the organization. Executives are responsible for the recruitment, selection, training, and development of personnel, and other personnel actions. The recent expansion of the space exploration program, for example, required the National Aeronautics and Space Administration to recruit 2,200 highly trained scientists and engineers to man its laboratories. Although certain personnel activities are performed by the central personnel agency, the major responsibility for personnel administration rests upon department executives.

6. Budget activities and administer finance. Budgeting and financial controls are among the most important functions of management. In preparing the budget, executives review the work programs and the relative needs of the various activities, and make key decisions concerning future operations. They are responsible not only for the preparation of sound work programs and budgets to carry on assigned activities, but also for securing the support of the central budget office, the chief executive, and the legislative body. Executives are also responsible for the execution of the budget, that is, for expenditures, accounting, and financial administration.

7. Control administrative activities and operations. Control requires accurate and up-to-date information about performance, including statistics on the work units performed, which are compared with goals, accepted standards, and unit costs. Without such standards statistics on performance have little significance. Adequate statistics and reports on operations, carefully analyzed, enable executives to evaluate accomplishments and take corrective steps when needed.

8. Make decisions and issue orders. The skillful executive utilizes his staff resources in decision making. Members of the staff analyze and evaluate problems calling for decisions, review the issues, consider alternative courses of action, forecast probable results, and prepare specific plans to carry out recommended decisions. Care is taken to assure adequate consultation and, if possible, to arrive at a consensus before decisions are reached. Timing is important, for the staff must be prepared to accept and carry out decisions when they are issued.

9. Represent the department or agency in external relations. This is largely the function of the head of a department and his chief assistants, who speak for the department, explain and defend its policies and legislative proposals, defend it from attacks, and accept responsibility for its administration. The head of a Federal department devotes a large part of his time to external relations—to conferences with the President, members of Congress, party leaders, and organized interest groups. He is frequently called upon to testify before congressional committees and delivers many public addresses.

EXECUTIVE LEADERSHIP   Equally or more important than the tasks of management that have been described above is the executive leadership of an organization. Leadership determines the spirit of an organization, the morale and motivation of its employees, and makes the difference between successful and unsuccessful performance. It is exercised not by the performance of individual tasks of management, but rather by the manner in which all executive functions are performed, and particularly the relations between executives, supervisors, and the rank and file of employees. Leadership depends upon the ability of executives at various levels to inspire the confidence and respect of their subordinates; to elicit their enthusiasm, loyalty, identification with the organization and its aims, and devotion to their duties. The most effective leader has a sincere belief in and devotion to the objectives of the program which he administers, and is able to transmit his enthusiasm to subordinates and employees.

Leadership creates a spirit of cooperation and teamwork throughout the organization. The effective leader sets high standards of integrity and performance and instills in his subordinates a pride in their work. "Leadership makes the difference between an outstanding performance and a mediocre one—the difference between a success and failure. Leadership combined with executive direction more than anything else determines and affects the attitude and spirit of people in an organization."[12]

Recent studies of human relations in industry and government have shattered many former notions about the forms of supervision and incentives that are most effective. They indicate, for example, that the use of financial rewards and the threat of disciplinary action are relatively ineffective, while supervision based upon an understanding of human relations and the desire of employees for individual recognition and satisfying conditions of work is more effective. Supervisors who demonstrate a genuine interest in their employees and their problems, and who encourage their participation in work planning and

[12] Matthias E. Lukens, "Practicing Management Theory," *Public Administration Review*, vol. 18, p. 224, 1958.

decisions are the most successful. General supervision has been found to be more effective than close supervision in most work situations. An informal, friendly environment, open channels of communication, and the awarding of praise when praise is earned are conducive to high levels of morale and production. Every employee consciously or unconsciously demands ego-satisfaction and a feeling of personal security which is derived from being treated as an individual person and from being recognized for his worth. Employees normally desire to be accepted into the work group. The executive as well as the supervisor needs to have, in addition to administrative and technical ability, a deep understanding of human behavior, of the aspirations, sentiments, and motivation of individual employees; skill in interpersonal relations; ability to communicate; and a genuine interest in the welfare and advancement of associates.[13]

Review Questions

1. Why is organization important in achieving high standards of administration?

2. Give an analysis and evaluation of the several elements of organization.

3. What are the characteristics of bureaucracy (big organization) found by Max Weber? Consider the significance of each characteristic. Is it applicable to big organization today?

4. How do the recent sociological studies of organization differ from the older studies by students of public administration? What are the values and limitations of each approach?

5. What is meant by "informal organization"? How does it modify formal organization?

6. What are the advantages and weaknesses of the following types of overhead organization: single head, commission, government corporation?

7. Review critically and thoughtfully the public administration "model" of organization.

[13] See Rensis Likert, *New Patterns of Management,* McGraw-Hill Book Company, Inc., New York, 1961, including a bibliography of the extensive literature on human relations in industry and government.

8. What is the distinction between "political executives" and "career executives"?

9. What are the major tasks of management? Consider each carefully.

10. Discuss executive leadership and its function in administration.

THE PUBLIC SERVICE

Chapter 3

Government today is the nation's largest employer. In 1960, governments at all levels in the United States employed 8.8 million civilian persons. The Federal government employed 2.4 million, or 27.5 per cent of the total; the states employed 1.6 million, or 18.1 per cent; and local government, including school districts, employed 4.8 million, or 54.4 per cent. In the 14 years following World War II—from 1946 to 1960—the number of state employees increased from 804,000 to 1.6 million, or 100 per cent, and local employees increased from 2.7 to 4.8 million, or 73 per cent. In contrast, the number of Federal civilian employees in 1960 was approximately the same as in 1946—2.4 million.[1]

During the last quarter of a century profound changes have taken place in the character of the Federal public service, as well as in that of the states and local governments. Formerly the large majority of government employees, apart from those in education, were engaged in clerical work, carrying the mail, maintaining law and order, and performing custodial duties in government institutions and hospitals. In the public image, government employees consisted largely of clerks, policemen, letter carriers, and others performing routine tasks that required little education or training. The common impression prevailed that government employees usually had "soft" jobs requiring little initiative or enterprise, and could not be fired.

Such images of the government worker bear little resemblance to the civil servant in the sixties. The majority of positions in the Federal government of today were unknown prior to World War II. The changes in state and local government have been almost as sweeping. Apart from the postal service, only one worker out of seven in the Federal government is engaged in clerical work. Three million public employees in 1960, or one out of every three, were engaged in education; a million civilian employees were engaged in national defense; and the third largest group, 850,000, were employed in public health and hospitals.

Governments today employ persons of practically every known profession, occupation, and field of specialization. The Federal government employs more scientists, engineers, economists, lawyers, statisticians, accountants, foresters, agricultural specialists, geologists, meteorologists, physicians, nurses, and still other categories of specialists than any other employer. The number of scientists and engineers employed by the Federal government increased from 13,631 in 1931 to 120,990 in 1958. The number of physical scientists and mathematicians increased from 2,758 in 1931 to 25,475 in 1954.[2] The Federal service includes more than 10,000 separate classes of position, while that of the states and cities includes most occupations and professions, ranging from apiary inspector to zoologist. Formerly governments recruited few employees from the colleges and professional schools; today many

[1] U.S. Bureau of the Census, *Government Employment: 1960*, Mar. 31, 1961, p. 6.
[2] *Scientists and Engineers in the Federal Government*, National Science Foundation, NSF 61-48, October, 1956.

graduates of universities and professional schools enter the public service.

These sweeping changes in the public service at all levels of government are due to the great changes that have taken place in government functions. Many of the most important government activities today did not exist a generation ago. As new functions have been assumed, older functions have been expanded and become more complex and technical, requiring highly qualified and trained personnel. The state and local governments today are carrying on programs of a size and complexity that were undreamed of a quarter of a century ago. No longer can it be said, as Andrew Jackson stated more than a century ago, that the duties of public office are so plain and simple that men of intelligence can quickly learn to perform them.

Modern government requires the services of many persons of outstanding ability for its many specialized and managerial positions, as well as competent employees for more routine work in the lower grades. It needs also personnel policies and administrative practices that will make it a model employer. If it is to perform efficiently its increased functions in an industrial, urban society, it must be able to recruit and retain its fair share of persons of outstanding ability, and to offer them rewarding careers, salaries that are competitive with those in business and industry, opportunities to engage in satisfying and creative work, advancement according to their abilities, and public recognition and esteem.

This is the challenge of the public service today. The central question concerning public personnel administration is: Are the conditions of employment, compensation, and career opportunities in the Federal government, and in the states and local governments, adequate to attract, to challenge, and to hold a fair share of the ablest graduates of our colleges and universities? A survey of personnel administration conducted in 1961 by the Municipal Manpower Commission and seven cooperating organizations in 221 cities, including 60 metropolitan areas, reached the conclusion that in nearly every respect local personnel practices failed to measure up to the task of providing sufficient numbers of adequately qualified administrative, professional, and technical personnel. The Commission reported that "the prevailing philosophy of personnel administration in most local governments is not based on the need for an adequate share of this scarce and vital talent. . . . The personnel practices—recruitment, compensation, and career development—of local governments are unequal to the task. . . ." It also found that personnel administration in many local governments is "artificially separated from, and independent of, the chief executive."[3]

Personnel administration in the Federal government and in the large majority of the states similarly fails to attract, develop, and retain a sufficient number of highly qualified personnel required today. Personnel standards and practices are not good enough. The concept of an independent civil service system, separate from management and designed primarily to prevent patronage appointments rather than to assist executive officers in personnel management, is outmoded.

DISTINGUISHING CHARACTERISTICS OF THE PUBLIC SERVICE

Several terms commonly used in discussing public personnel administration need to be defined.

The *public service* refers to all public employees, but in this chapter is limited to civilian employees. The *civil service* is commonly used to refer to government employees who are appointed on the basis of examinations given by the Civil Service Commission and who acquire civil service status after the probationary period. The *merit system* refers to a personnel system in which appointments and other personnel actions are based on the qualifications or merit of the individual. A civil service system may or may not be a true merit system, depending on its administration, while some personnel systems not under civil service (e.g., TVA and the Foreign Service) are administered on the basis of merit. A *career system* is a public service in which employees ordinarily enter early in life and continue until retirement. The *spoils system* exists when persons are appointed to public office as a reward for political services.

Although public and private personnel administration have much in common, there are significant differences that make the problems and tasks of personnel management in the public service different from those in private employment. Governments require unquestioned loyalty of their employees. In the early history of the Republic, President Washington took pains to see to it that only persons who were loyal to the new Constitution were appointed to the principal offices. After the government had become well established, the loyalty of citizens who accepted Federal employment was assumed without spe-

[3] *Governmental Manpower for Tomorrow's Cities*, McGraw-Hill Book Company, Inc., New York, 1962, p. 53.

cial inquiry. A hundred and fifty years later, however, when the threat of Communism aroused the fears of the public, loyalty investigations were instituted.

Because the state is sovereign its employees are subject to various restrictions on their activities. One restriction circumscribes the right of public employees to form unions and the activities which may be carried on by such unions. Public employees in the United States are usually prohibited by law from engaging in strikes, and unions of public employees almost invariably disclaim the right to strike.

Public employees are also restricted in engaging in political activities. Under the former spoils system, which still prevails in some areas, public employees are expected to contribute to the party in office and to take an active part in political campaigns. This prostitution of the public service for partisan purposes led to civil service regulations and later to the Hatch Act prohibiting public employees from actively participating in political campaigns. There are many who think that the present Federal restrictions are too severe and unwisely deprive public servants of their right as citizens to take an active part in public affairs. The political sterilization of over eight million Federal, state, and local employees and the members of their families is regrettable.

Another characteristic of the public service in a democratic society is that it is representative of the entire population, drawn from all geographic areas, all racial and religious groups, and all economic classes and walks of life. This is one of the strengths of the American public service, though pockets of discrimination against minority groups and, for certain positions, against women still prevail.

A closely related principle is that equality of treatment shall be accorded to all applicants for the public service and to all employees after they have entered the service. Open, competitive examinations and the appointment of the candidates who stand highest on the registers are based on this principle. The principle of equality, however, is qualified by granting preference to veterans of foreign wars. Until recently veterans' preference was accorded only in entrance examinations; after entrance into the Federal service, veterans and nonveterans were treated alike. The Veterans' Preference Act of 1945, however, accords veterans continuing rights over nonveterans and in this respect departs from the historical practice.

A supposed characteristic of the public service, especially under civil service laws, is that public employees, after the probationary period, cannot be discharged except for gross inefficiency or misconduct. Public employment normally provides greater security to employees than private employment, but today private employers' freedom to discharge employees is limited by management-labor agreements. The widely held belief that incompetent public employees cannot be fired is in part a myth, but civil service regulations and procedures often make discharge difficult.

Public personnel administration has undergone substantial changes in the last 30 years. Civil service commissions formerly acted largely as police agencies, watching over the departments to prevent patronage appointments instead of assisting them in personnel management. Until recent decades civil service commissions were limited to conducting entrance examinations, and personnel management (such as it was) was carried on by clerks in the departments. Fortunately the negative, police type of civil service has been superseded in some states and cities by a new spirit of personnel management in which the central personnel agency, headed by a single director of personnel, works closely with department executives in improving personnel standards and policies. The more progressive personnel agencies today carry on comprehensive personnel programs, including positive recruitment, examinations, training, promotion, classification and pay, employee relations, and other activities.

Personnel administration in government is being increasingly de-centralized to the operating departments and conducted as an aspect of management. No longer is it regarded as a clerical activity, but has come to be recognized as an important function of management. Personnel officers today are devoting increasing attention to motivation and employee morale, to the training of supervisors, and to advising executives on personnel policies. The trend toward personnel management, however, has been uneven. Many personnel agencies still cling to the older, negative, police concept and in many communities the term "civil service" evokes an image of a wooden, unimaginative public service filled with incompetent employees who cannot be discharged.

The improvement of public personnel administration in this country has had to overcome serious difficulties. Patronage appointments still are the rule for many higher appointments, as in the postal service, and limit the opportunities of career employees for advancement. The widely held but erroneous belief that government is always less efficient than private business and offers fewer opportunities for advancement and satisfying careers discourages many able young men and women from entering the public service. Low salaries, especially in the upper grades, handicaps government in recruiting and retaining competent personnel. Residence requirements often handicap local governments in recruiting persons with professional training and experience.

ORGANIZATION FOR PERSONNEL ADMINISTRATION

Although business and industry invariably use a single director of personnel, who is responsible to the general manager, civil service commissions are generally used in government. This form of organization has been adopted in the belief that a commission provides greater protection than a single director against patronage appointments. The results have generally been unsatisfactory. Civil service commissions often regard their function as that of preventing patronage appointments rather than aiding the departments in recruiting able personnel and maintaining conditions of employment that make the public service attractive to well-qualified persons. Most politically appointed civil service commissioners have had little or no training and experience in personnel administration.

Public administration authorities today are generally agreed that personnel administration is a function of management and therefore a single director of personnel who is responsible to the chief executive should be used. A single director is better able than a commission to serve the needs of the departments and to aid them in developing high personnel standards. Although the trend is for greater use of single directors, most state and local governments continue to use civil service commissions. The Chairman of the Federal Civil Service Commission, it should be noted, is in charge of administration, assisted by an executive director. The Commission as a body is limited to decisions on policies and hearing appeals.

CLASSIFICATION AND PAY

In the early history of civil service, positions were seldom classified according to duties and responsibilities. Position titles often had little relation to the duties performed. Many positions, identical in duties and responsibilities, were classified under various titles, and persons performing the same tasks were often paid widely varying salaries. The failure to classify positions according to their duties and responsibilities made it impossible for the legislative body to adopt a rational salary policy and hampered almost every aspect of personnel administration.

Since about 1920 the practice has developed of classifying positions—not employees—according to their duties and responsibilities, and the qualifications required. Classification of positions requires a detailed study and analysis of each position. Ordinarily the employees are required to fill in a questionnaire describing the various tasks which they perform, the amount of time devoted to each, the supervision which they receive, and other details. Desk audits are conducted to verify the details when necessary. On the basis of this information, each position is assigned to the appropriate class.

One of the greatest weaknesses of the public service, as a rule, is the absence of a realistic pay policy for the higher grades. Employees in the lower and middle grades and in the skilled trades are usually paid wages equal to or even higher than those paid by private employers, but employees in the higher grades are paid substantially less. A survey conducted by the Bureau of Labor Statistics in 1960 indicated that employees of the Federal government in grades GS 12 to 15 received salaries of $9,735 to $14,705, while employees in similar positions in business firms received from $11,125 to $20,175, or 14 to 37 per cent higher. A similar survey conducted by the Civil Service Commission for the three top civil service grades—GS 16, 17, and 18 —indicated that in comparison with government salaries ranging from $15,255 to $18,500, twenty-one large corporations were paying for similar positions from $20,000 to $45,000, or 60 to 115 per cent higher. The salary scales paid by state and local governments are generally lower than those of the Federal government, though many city managers and school superintendents receive salaries of from $25,000 to $30,000.

The failure of government to pay salaries in the higher grades that are comparable to those paid by private employers for comparable work is false economy, for it hampers government in recruiting well-qualified personnel and causes it to lose many of its most valuable employees to private industry. Formerly government provided greater fringe benefits than private employers, but this is no longer true. A more realistic pay policy is necessary if government is to be able to recruit its fair share of scientists, professional persons, and those with managerial talents needed to direct its complex and vitally important programs.[4]

RECRUITMENT AND SELECTION

Positive recruiting is needed to bring the opportunities in the public service to the attention of qualified persons. Increasingly, personnel agencies and operating departments conduct recruiting drives, visiting colleges and universities to interview graduating seniors during the spring and make definite offers of employment on the spot. Attractive brochures are published by the more progressive personnel agencies indicating the career opportunities. For certain types of clerical positions, examinations are conducted continuously, and candidates who receive satisfactory scores are offered positions without delay.

In the public service candidates are usually rated on the basis of written examinations, though some use is also made of oral tests and performance examinations for certain types of positions. The great reliance placed upon written examinations is due to the basic policy that entrance into the public service shall be open and competitive. All persons who meet the qualifications and residence requirements are entitled to take the examinations, and those who receive the highest scores are placed at the top of the registers for appointment, though individual candidates may be passed over by the departments. Written examinations are not necessarily the best means for judging the qualifications and abilities of candidates, but they can be objectively scored and thus charges of favoritism and political influence are avoided. Short-answer questions are almost invariably used, and many personnel agencies use electronic scoring machines.

Written examinations may be classified into two broad categories: (1) achievement tests, which measure the knowledge and skills of candidates, and (2) aptitude tests, which measure the capacity of candidates to acquire the necessary knowledge and skills. Civil service examinations are usually of the achievement type, which attempt to determine whether the candidate has the qualifications necessary for the performance of the particular job, but aptitude tests are increasingly used. The capacity of the candidate to learn is often more important than his knowledge and skills when he takes the examination.

Persons appointed from civil service registers are required to serve

[4] See John J. Corson, "Comparable Pay for Comparable Work," *Public Administration Review,* vol. XXI, pp. 198–205, 1961.

a probationary period, usually six months to a year, during which they may be summarily dismissed. Although the probationary period permits the weeding out of unsatisfactory employees, in practice relatively few are dismissed.

TRAINING AND PROMOTION

In-service training of employees is widely used by government departments to prepare employees for better performance of their duties, to equip them for new tasks or new procedures, and to qualify them for promotion. Government is rapidly undergoing changes in methods and techniques, which require the constant training of employees. The central personnel agency provides assistance and leadership in developing effective training programs, but the responsibility for training rests primarily on the operating departments. The Federal Training Act of 1958 authorizes executive departments to conduct training either on or off the job, and to pay for employee training at universities and other institutions.

Various methods are used to select employees for promotion. Examinations are widely used in the public service but are subject to the limitation that they cannot accurately measure those traits of character and leadership required for effective supervision. Seniority is often accorded undue weight. Long service in a subordinate position rarely qualifies the incumbent for the duties and responsibilities of the next higher position. Service ratings are notoriously unreliable and hence a poor criterion for promotion. In the Federal government promotions are usually made on the recommendation of the supervisory staff. This method is perhaps, on the whole, more satisfactory than written examinations, for it permits the choice to be made on the basis of extended observation of persons considered for promotion, but it is subject to abuse and favoritism unless it is carefully administered.

EMPLOYEE ORGANIZATIONS

Public employees have formed unions and other organizations to represent them in their dealings with management and the legislative body, and for other purposes. More than 90 per cent of the postal employees of the Federal government belong to unions, most of which are affiliated with the AFL-CIO, and about one-fourth of other Federal employees belong to unions—approximately the same proportion as in private employment. Employees of state and local government belong to a wide variety of unions and other organizations. Apart from employees in the skilled trades, however, only a small number belong to unions affiliated with the AFL-CIO. Some of the largest unions of state and local employees (e.g., the International Association of Fire Fighters) are unaffiliated with the national labor movement.

In several states and the larger metropolitan areas there are semi-professional associations of public employees which perform many of the functions of a labor union. An outstanding example is the California State Employees Association, which carries on various activities for the benefit of its members, fights to uphold the merit system in state government, conducts training institutes, and wields considerable influence in the state legislature on personnel matters. The high standards of personnel administration in the California state government are due in no small part to the vigorous and well-directed activities of the Association.

Should unions of public employees have the same rights as other unions to bargain collectively and to strike? Government executives ordinarily decline to enter into collective bargaining with employee unions on the ground that such action is not authorized by law. Wages, hours, and conditions of work are usually fixed by the legislative body. A few lower courts have held that since the state is a sovereign body, government cannot enter into collective bargaining with unions of employees.

Instead of bargaining with management, unions of public employees present their demands for higher wages and better working conditions directly to the legislature and carry on lobbying activities to secure their acceptance. They resort to political rather than economic pressure, and it is with the legislature that they are able to exert the greatest influence.

It is generally believed that public employees have no right to strike against government, which represents all the people. Several states have enacted laws outlawing strikes by public employees. The constitutions and bylaws of most unions of public employees expressly disavow the right to strike. Because of the restrictions placed upon its employees not to engage in strikes, government has a duty to give its employees an opportunity to present their claims, and to treat them fairly, making it unnecessary for them to resort to the ultimate weapon of organized labor. Yet many work stoppages and strikes do occur in the public service, usually as a last resort by employees who believe that they have not been accorded fair and just treatment and resort to the strike in order to bring their claims to public attention.

VETERANS' PREFERENCE

Preference in initial appointment to the public service has long been accorded to veterans of foreign wars. Following the Civil War, veterans of the Union forces who had service-connected disabilities were given preference, provided their qualifications were equal to those of available nonveterans. Relatively few veterans qualified for preference under these provisions. It was not until after World War I that preference was given to all veterans of a foreign war and to the wives and widows of disabled veterans. Ten extra points on examinations were given to disabled veterans, and those who passed the examinations with the benefit of these extra points were placed at the top of the registers. Other veterans received a bonus of five points on examinations. Large numbers of veterans took advantage of these preference provisions between the two world wars.

As World War II came to an end, Congress enacted the Veterans' Preference Act of 1945, which wrote into law all the previous executive orders granting preference to veterans (thus making it difficult to revise the rules if they worked badly) and extended the preference accorded to veterans. The rule giving absolute preference to disabled veterans placed many poorly qualified disabled veterans at the top of registers and thus made it impossible to appoint better-qualified candidates, most of whom were veterans. Fortunately, the law was subsequently modified to require disabled veterans to receive passing scores before being given 10 extra points and placed at the top of the registers. Even so, the absolute preference accorded to disabled veterans, their wives and widows, has little to commend it as a personnel policy.

In an earlier age when the functions of government were relatively simple, and few government employees were required to have expert qualifications, veterans' preference had less harmful effects on the public service than it does today. Government requires large numbers of persons with high qualifications and technical training for which veterans' preference is a poor substitute.

LOYALTY AND SECURITY

The loyalty of Federal employees became a national issue in the years following World War II, owing to widely publicized charges (which were never substantiated) that many Communists and Communist sympathizers were employed by the government. For the first time in the history of the country an investigation of the loyalty of all employees in the Federal service was instituted, and a few were dismissed on loyalty grounds. Now that the issue has largely passed and we may look back in retrospect, it is clear that the charges were grossly exaggerated and the actual danger of subversion was slight. The attacks on the loyalty of Federal employees, often politically inspired, did much to lower the Federal service in public esteem and to make it unattractive as a career at a time when the government increasingly needed highly qualified employees. Fortunately, state and local government employees were not subjected to similar attacks.

For 150 years prior to 1939 it had been assumed that citizens who applied for Federal employment were loyal. Only in rare cases was it considered necessary to investigate their loyalty. The Pendleton Act of 1883 prohibited inquiries concerning the political or religious views of applicants. In 1939, however, a rider to the Hatch Act (which prohibited Federal employees from engaging in political activities) prohibited the employment of any person who "advocates or belongs to an organization that advocates the overthrow of the government by force or violence." This phraseology was used because it was believed that the direct outlawing of the employment of members of the Communist Party would be held to be unconstitutional. All Federal employees were required to take an oath that they did not come under this ban, and the Civil Service Commission began the practice of making loyalty investigations of new employees.

During World War II the defense departments were authorized to discharge summarily, without regard to civil service laws and regulations, any employee whose removal was deemed in the national interest. Investigations were made of a limited number of persons engaged in war activities, but it was not deemed necessary or desirable to investigate the loyalty of all employees.

In 1947, however, President Truman, yielding to demands voiced in Congress, issued an Executive order providing for an investigation of the loyalty of all Federal employees. The order established careful procedures to safeguard the rights of employees, including the right of a hearing on charges of disloyalty and an appeal to a central review board under the Civil Service Commission.

Nevertheless, loyalty investigations under the Truman order were seriously criticized. Employees who appeared before review boards were not permitted to examine the evidence against them, but were provided only with summaries. Adverse witnesses were not required to appear at the hearing and be cross-examined; even their names were not known to the review board. The program was widely criticized because employees were subject to discharge under the novel doctrine of "guilt by association" and on the basis of secret testimony of faceless witnesses. The program was also criticized for not being stringent enough, and demands were voiced in Congress for the removal of more Federal employees who were alleged to be Communists or Communist sympathizers.

Shortly after taking office in 1953, President Eisenhower instituted a new and more stringent loyalty and security program, as he had promised to do during the campaign. Dismissals for security and loyalty reasons were combined into a single program. This meant that a person could be dismissed as a poor security risk (as for talking too freely or drinking in excess) without any evidence of disloyalty. The new Executive order required another review of the loyalty of many employees who had previously been cleared. No longer were employees permitted an appeal to a central appeals board.

The Eisenhower loyalty-security program was subsequently modified by several Supreme Court decisions, one holding that summary dismissal of employees as poor security risks was authorized by statute only for "sensitive" positions.[5] After this decision, many employees previously dismissed were reinstated. The New York Bar Association and the American Assembly issued reports criticizing the loyalty-security program because of its denial of basic civil rights to Federal employees and its injurious effects on the Federal service, and called for revisions which would provide protection against disloyalty and subversion without harming the civil service. Fortunately, the furor over the loyalty of Federal employees has largely passed.

CONTROL OF THE PUBLIC SERVICE

In democratic governments it is essential that suitable controls be established to ensure that high standards of personnel are maintained, that public employees perform their tasks faithfully, loyally, and efficiently, and to safeguard against abuses of authority. Various controls over the Federal civil service are exercised by the bureaus and departments, the Civil Service Commission, the President, and the Congress. The bureaus and departments, which are primarily responsible for personnel administration, are today equipped with well-staffed personnel offices. These offices assist the operating officials in per-

[5] *Cole v. Young*, 351 U.S. 536 (1956).

sonnel matters and have the responsibility of seeing to it that personnel standards are maintained and policies, laws, and regulations are observed. The Civil Service Commission sets standards of personnel administration, issues regulations, inspects the personnel administration in the departments, renders technical assistance, and advises the President and Congress on personnel policies.

The President is responsible for providing leadership in personnel administration throughout the government. He recommends personnel policies and legislation to Congress and issues executive orders regulating the civil service. President Eisenhower, for example, actively supported training legislation which was passed by Congress in 1958, and urged Congress to create a commission to inquire into Federal pay plans and to recommend comprehensive legislation, but Congress failed to act. President Kennedy submitted a special message to Congress in February, 1962, recommending a substantial pay revision to bring government salaries into line with those paid in private industry.

Congress exercises control over the Federal service primarily through statutes which establish personnel policies and authorize and regulate personnel activities. It also exercises control by conducting investigations and in voting appropriations. Formerly Congress legislated only upon broad personnel policies, leaving detailed regulations to the President and the Civil Service Commission, but in recent decades it has legislated on almost all aspects of personnel administration. This practice has been criticized because it deprives the President and executive officers of needed discretion and tends to freeze personnel procedures in a rigid pattern that soon becomes outmoded. Congress, however, has shown no disposition to return to its former practice of legislating only on broad policies.

THE FUTURE OF THE PUBLIC SERVICE

If government is to be able to perform the increasingly complex functions placed on it today and cope effectively with the problems of an age of automation and revolutionary change, outmoded concepts of civil service must be supplanted by modern concepts and standards of personnel management. The major responsibility for personnel administration lies not with the central personnel agency but with the operating departments. If it is to serve management effectively, the personnel agency must become *a part* of management, not *apart* from management. The spirit of personnel administration must be changed from negative restrictions and prohibitions to that of positive goals and standards. The use of bipartisan, independent civil service commissions, separate from management, was dictated by concepts and conditions that are no longer applicable.

Many of the present civil service practices must be discarded and more effective policies and procedures adopted. Government must seek out and recruit qualified and promising persons, utilize testing in a more flexible manner, discard restrictions and preferences that are contrary to the merit system, accord its employees equal rights with private employees, and afford them adequate opportunities for development and growth. An able public service with high motivation and devotion to duty is the first requirement of competent and effective public administration.

Review Questions

1. Discuss the major changes that have taken place in the public employment in the last quarter of a century.

2. Define: public service, civil service, merit system, career service, spoils system, political executives, career executives.

3. What are the distinguishing characteristics of the public service?

4. Discuss the merits of an independent civil service commission versus a single director of personnel responsible to the chief executive.

5. What are the principal handicaps of government in recruiting and retaining qualified personnel in competition with industry?

6. Should governments enter into collective bargaining with employee unions? Should strikes of public employees be permitted?

7. What are the arguments for and against veterans' preference?

8. Discuss the effects of loyalty investigations on the Federal service.

ADMINISTERING TRADITIONAL FEDERAL FUNCTIONS

Chapter 4

It is in the Federal government that such factors as population growth, urbanization, industrialization, the cold war, this country's involvement in international affairs, and the rapid advance in technology have induced the greatest growth in the size and scope of government. This growth is seen in the evolution of the administrative organization of the Federal government.

THE PRESIDENT AND HIS STAFF

The President has available, first, an immediate personal staff in the White House.

Secondly, there are five agencies which, with the White House staff, make up the Executive Office of the President. Finally, two independent agencies—the Civil Service Commission and the General Services Administration—complete his staff. The organization of his staff is shown in the figure on page 54.

THE WHITE HOUSE OFFICE Enveloped in the loneliness of the highest office, confronted by the overwhelming variety of problems welling up throughout the nation, and handicapped by the inability of even "big men" serving as department and agency heads to speak their minds to their Chief Executive, most Presidents have needed able men to help them winnow fact from masses of conflicting prejudice, selfishness, and partisanship. Hence, Woodrow Wilson had Colonel House; Franklin D. Roosevelt, Louis Howe and later Harry Hopkins; Harry S. Truman, John Steelman; Dwight D. Eisenhower, Sherman Adams; and John F. Kennedy, "Mac" Bundy and Ted Sorenson.

In addition, each President has needed a variety of assistants to aid him with the flow of work that results from his relations with the Congress, the press, the departments, the agencies, the party, and the public. Such work includes preparation for meetings, handling telephone talks, and writing speeches and papers, formal and informal. Under Presidents Truman, Eisenhower, and Kennedy assistants included a special counsel, an appointments secretary, a press secretary, several administrative or special assistants, a chief clerk, and requisite secretaries and clerks.[1]

Until 1939, the President was provided with only a very small staff. Then, upon the recommendation of President Roosevelt's Committee on Administrative Management, the White House staff was substantially increased. Under President Truman, the White House staff totaled 22; under President Eisenhower, the size of the staff almost doubled—to 43; under President Kennedy, the staff numbered 29 in 1962.

THE BUREAU OF THE BUDGET This agency serves as "the President's programing staff." The Budget and Accounting Act of 1921 fixed on the President the duty of preparing annual estimates of receipts and

---

[1] A discussion of the ways in which a President uses his personal staff and how that staff defines his concept of administration may be found in Laurin Henry's *Presidential Transitions* (The Brookings Institution, Washington, D.C., 1960).

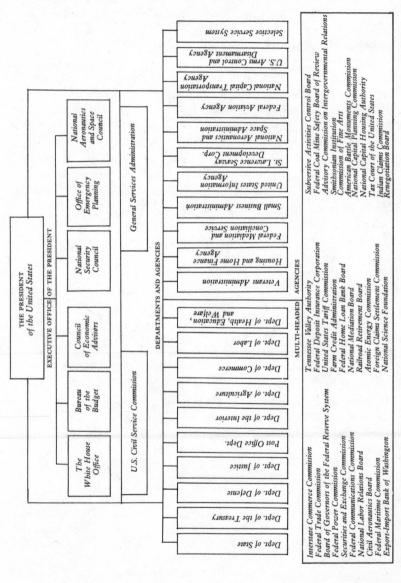

The structure of the Federal government.

expenses. But it was the depression of the thirties that made clear that government spending and taxation is a force that can be used to influence the economy and that the budget is the President's tool for shaping his whole program rather than simply an accounting operation.

Members of the Bureau's staff devote their time largely to studying what goes on in each major field of government (e.g., health, education, and welfare, or foreign economic affairs). They review the annual spending programs proposed by each department and agency and the bills which the departments or agencies propose for presentation to Congress or which have been introduced by members of Congress. They continually appraise what goes on in each department and agency, and are concerned with the relationships between departments and agencies. In short, they assist the President in making a consistent whole of his program and in seeing that it is carried out.

The Director of the Bureau, in assisting the President to prepare the annual budget of the United States and in evaluating legislation that is to be considered by the Congress, is his principal adviser on the government's various programs. Each strong budget director serves essentially as the President's "chief of staff"; the weaker ones content themselves (as long as they last) with being the "watchdog of the treasury," that is, striving to keep expenditures down.

THE COUNCIL OF ECONOMIC ADVISERS Created by the Employment Act of 1946 when the American economy was making extensive adjustments to effect a transition from war to peace, this agency seeks to aid the President in maintaining a high level of employment and economic stability.

The Council includes three members appointed by the President. Its staff of about twenty economists and statisticians is supplemented by approximately twenty consultants, most of whom are economists on the faculties of leading colleges and universities. The Council advises the President and the heads of executive departments and agencies and explains to the Congress and to the public the general economic strategy of the President's program. The Council members and their staff are in day-to-day consultation with members of the White House staff and officials of the executive agencies. Their work focuses on the review of monetary developments and problems, on projections of economic activity, on the coordination of economic, budgetary, and revenue estimates, and on consideration of the economic effects of each Federal program (e.g., the housing program or the small business program).

THE OFFICE OF EMERGENCY PLANNING (OEP) The lineal organizational descendant of the National Security Resources Board established shortly after World War II, the OEP assists the President in planning for the use, in the event of war, of this country's natural resources, its manpower, its transport system, its productive capacity—the mills, plants, and factories—and such vital institutions as the banking system. It is engaged in stockpiling strategic materials, in controlling exports and imports of such essential materials as petroleum, and in planning what might be required if war comes again.

THE NATIONAL SECURITY COUNCIL During the terms of Presidents Truman, Eisenhower, and Kennedy the Special Assistant for National Security Council Affairs has been an especially important member of the President's staff, and the National Security Council an organizational instrument of great significance. The Council, created in 1947, is made up of the President, the Vice President, the Secretary of Defense, the Secretary of State, and the Director of the Office of Emergency Planning.

"The real worth of the Council to a President," as the Senate Subcommittee on National Policy Machinery aptly pointed out, "lies in being an accustomed forum . . . where the President can receive from his department and agency heads a full exposition of policy alternatives available to him and, in turn, give them clear-cut guidance for action."[2] When it has served this purpose, as during the Kennedy administration, it has tended to supersede the Cabinet, which with its larger membership and fewer common problems does not provide a forum that stimulates equally full and frank exchange of opinion. The Council has been least useful when its staff formalized unduly the processes by which problems were presented and discussion was controlled.

The Central Intelligence Agency is an organ of the Council. It collects, coordinates, and evaluates the intelligence essential to framing our military, international, and economic policies. Its clandestine activ-

[2] "Organizing for National Security," Volume 3, *Staff Reports and Recommendations; Inquiry of the Subcommittee on National Policy Machinery,* Sen. Henry M. Jackson, Chairman for the Committee on Government Operations, U.S. Senate (1961), p. 38.

ities, such as planning the U-2 flights and assisting refugee Cubans in planning and training a force to free their homeland, are necessarily carried on in the greatest of secrecy. The Agency is, hence, not required, as are other Federal agencies, to report publicly its activities and expenditures, the number and duties of its employees, or even the salaries paid.[3]

THE OFFICE OF SCIENCE AND TECHNOLOGY The establishment of this office in 1962 was one of a series of organizational steps that successive Presidents took following World War II to make available competent advice on problems arising out of the impact of science on government. In addition to advising the President and coordinating the scientific activities of the Federal departments and agencies, a major function of this Office is to do for the Congress as well as for the President what Winston Churchill said that Lord Cherwell did for him—"decipher the signals from the experts on the far horizons and explain to me in lucid, homely terms what the issues were."

THE CIVIL SERVICE COMMISSION This is a bipartisan body of three members appointed by the President and confirmed by the Senate. It administers the civil service laws which govern the recruitment, compensation, dismissal, and retirement of all civil service employees. This means that its staff of approximately 3,600 men and women is continually working to find the workers that the departments and agencies need, to aid them in fixing the compensation for and in training such employees, and to meet the myriad of personnel problems which arise. In addition, the Civil Service Commission is the appeals agency to which employees turn when they believe they have been unjustly treated.

During much of the administration of President Eisenhower and during President Kennedy's early years in office, the Chairman of the Civil Service Commission was the President's special adviser on

---

[3] This freedom has attracted recurrent efforts in Congress to set up a Congressional "watchdog committee" to oversee operations of the CIA. These efforts have been persistently resisted. In alternative, the second Hoover Commission recommended that a "small, permanent, bipartisan commission, composed of members of both houses of the Congress and other public spirited citizens" be established to make periodic surveys of the "organization, functions, policies, and results of Government agencies handling foreign intelligence operations." "Intelligence Activities," *Report of the Commission on Organization of the Executive Branch of the Government*, June, 1955, p. 71.

personnel problems. In this capacity he served as an immediate member of the President's staff and assisted him in handling problems involving all Federal employees, i.e., those in the postal service, the Foreign Service, and other groups as well as those in the civil service. In addition, the President customarily has one or two assistants who help him find and "screen" people for the approximately 1,500 positions he fills by political appointment.

THE GENERAL SERVICES ADMINISTRATION The GSA, one of the largest agencies in the executive branch, is the Federal government's housekeeper. Its administrator sees to it that the physical requirements of the departments and agencies are met.

The GSA consists of five services: (1) the Public Buildings Service, with more than 20,000 employees, is engaged in providing buildings having more than 120 million square feet of working space (your home probably contains less than 2,000 square feet!) for Federal activities; (2) the Federal Supply Service buys annually more than 800 million dollars' worth of supplies that are in common use by all Federal departments and agencies (e.g., paper, desks); (3) the National Archives preserves all essential government records; (4) the Defense Materials Service procures (as directed by the OEP) and maintains the critical reserves of raw materials and industrial equipment which may be needed in the event of war; and (5) the Transportation and Public Utilities Service assists the departments in handling their transportation, communication, and public utility problems.

Every decision concerning an executive order, the budget of a department, proposed legislation, the appointment of a postmaster or marshal, or the construction of a new government building in a town far from Washington affects voters generally or the attitudes of specific groups (e.g., businessmen or veterans). Each such decision strengthens or weakens the President's popular support. It follows that the staff members of each of the agencies determine the very nature of the President's democratic leadership.

ADMINISTERING THE EXECUTIVE DEPARTMENTS

Most of the business of government—the collection of taxes, the enforcement of laws, the defense of the country, the delivery of the mails, the conduct of international relations, and the maintenance of our natural resources, is done by the executive departments. The 13 executive departments employed approximately 2.3 million civil employees during 1962. These departments, for purposes of analysis, comprise three groups.

The first group includes only the largest of the departments, the Department of Defense and its "subsidiaries"—the departments of the Army, Air Force, and Navy. The second group is made up of the departments concerned with the central and traditional business of government: Justice, Post Office, Treasury, and State. The third group includes five departments, each of which is engaged in "promoting" an important interest: Agriculture, Commerce, Interior, Labor, and Health, Education, and Welfare.

THE DEPARTMENT OF DEFENSE   The task of ensuring the security of this country for the foreseeable future requires the President to make decisions of unprecedented import: political decisions as to whether to increase the size of the armed forces; economic decisions concerning the size of the defense budget and what it will do to business in this country; international decisions relating to whether troops shall be sent to Congo, Laos, or Berlin; and life-and-death decisions as to when, if we must, we will go to war. The immensity of these decisions and the structure of the Department of Defense and its relationship with the departments of the Army, Air Force, and Navy will be discussed in a later chapter.

THE DEPARTMENT OF STATE   The administration of our nation's foreign affairs is a vastly different task from that assumed by Cordell Hull when he became Secretary of State in 1933. At that time the Department included only 4,500 employees, and the job consisted of facilitating political and economic relations with other countries of the world. The importance of the job then and now is reflected by the fact that the Secretary of State has always enjoyed a more direct, intimate, and continuous relationship with the President than has any other Cabinet member.

More recently, as the wealthiest and strongest nation in the free world, the United States has had to assume the great-power burdens which Great Britain carried for more than a century. And as technology has enabled jets, space communication, and missiles to shrink the world to a fraction of its size in the thirties, the Department's job has become more important than ever before.

The task of managing more than 38,000 employees engaged in germinating ideas and formulating and interpreting policies that will "fit" the problems we encounter in Addis Ababa or Zanzibar is infinitely more complex than that of producing a more tangible product or service. Moreover, the Department must coordinate the activities of more than 50 departments and agencies involved in foreign affairs. For example, it must coordinate the actions of the Tariff Commission in raising or lowering the duties on particular products, or the provision of information or fissionable material to a country under the "Atoms for Peace Program," with all other aspects of this country's relations with the foreign countries involved.

In addition, the methods as well as the substance of foreign affairs have changed. The tools of foreign affairs are no longer the striped trousers and skills of the diplomat. Our activities overseas require the expertise of the agricultural specialist, teacher, and sanitary engineer, who work in the back country of Afghanistan, Pakistan, and elsewhere. To achieve our objectives, the government makes loans to finance dams in Turkey, schools in Iran, and hospitals in Cambodia, and beams radio messages into and distributes publications in friendly and enemy countries alike. Hence, the Department of State guides and works with two important and related agencies: the U.S. Information Agency, which strives to tell the peoples of other countries what this country is like and what our goals are, and the Agency for International Development (AID), which makes loans and grants and provides "technical assistance" to each of many friendly or neutral countries.

THE DEPARTMENT OF THE TREASURY It administers, as its title implies, Federal taxes and customs, manages the public debts, coins and prints money, pays the government's bills, and keeps the government's accounts. In addition, it polices our coasts, controls the narcotics trade, supervises national banks, and controls this country's international financial affairs. These activities are carried on by the Internal Revenue Service (the largest unit within the Treasury, with more than 50,000 employees), the Bureau of Customs, the U.S. Coast Guard, the Bureau of the Mint, the Bureau of Narcotics, the Bureau of Engraving and Printing, the Office of the Comptroller of the Currency, and other units.

As the Secretary of State is the President's adviser on foreign affairs, the Secretary of the Treasury is his principal financial adviser. As such, his concern extends well beyond the walls of the Treasury Department. As the U.S. Governor of the International Bank, the Monetary Fund, and the Inter-American Bank, he is the country's spokesman in international finance.

As the chief financial officer within the Federal government, the Secretary of the Treasury works in close collaboration with the Director of the Bureau of the Budget on coordinating revenue and expenditure policies, with the Chairman of the Federal Reserve Board on debt and banking policies, with the Chairman of the Council of Economic Advisers and the Secretary of Commerce on the maintenance of economic stability, and with the Secretary of State on matters of international finance.

This is the comprehensive and complex administrative responsibility of the chief financial officer of the richest country in the world. And this is the sum of the tasks of more than 78,000 employees who serve under him in the Treasury.

THE DEPARTMENT OF JUSTICE   This department is the law office and police force of the Federal government. Over 60 per cent of its 30,000 employees are scattered throughout the United States in field offices of the Federal Bureau of Investigation, in Federal prisons, in offices of the Immigration and Naturalization Service, and in offices of the U.S. district attorneys and of the U.S. marshals associated with each of the Federal courts.

The Attorney General, the Federal government's chief legal officer, directs all litigation in which the Federal government is involved. In this task he is aided by seven assistant attorneys general, each of whom heads a division concerned with one type of legal problem. The Antitrust Division, with about 500 employees, is the largest of these divisions. The others are the Civil Rights, Internal Security, Criminal, Tax, Civil, and Lands divisions.

Momentous issues arise in these fields. In the antitrust field during the early sixties, among the most notable cases were those in which the government sued to force the Du Pont interests to sell all stock they held in the General Motors Corporation and in which it prosecuted manufacturers in the electrical equipment industry for price-fixing. The most momentous issue in the civil rights field during these years was segregation, and a succession of cases was fought by the government to establish the rights of Negroes to attend the same schools, use the same businesses, and eat at the same restaurants as whites.[4] Much of the litigation work of this department is routine, but many cases that it handles deal with the most vital issues of our time.

THE POST OFFICE DEPARTMENT This is a business that requires more than 560,000 employees and 35,000 post offices to deliver some 65 billion pieces of mail annually. Yet, to describe this department as a "business" is to prejudice a highly controversial issue. Is the postal service a public service that government provides, as it builds roads, or is it a service performed, at cost or at a profit, for those who use it, as some municipal governments distribute water to the homes of their residents?

The delivery of mail is important to each of us. But for some business interests—many advertisers, publishers, and mail-order houses —this service is of vital importance. Hence, the Postmaster General is the principal target of the lobbying efforts of such powerful groups as the American Newspaper Publishers' Association, the Magazine Publishers' Association, the Association of First-Class Mailers, and numerous others. Each has a vested interest in keeping postal rates down and in seeing to it that postal services are adapted to its particular needs.

Similarly, the Postmaster General and his colleagues are subject to the pressures of powerful organizations of the Department's employees. These include the National Association of Letter Carriers, the National Federation of Post Office Clerks, and the National Postal Transport Association. Recurrently, they seek higher earnings and improved conditions of work and strive to maintain personnel policies, such as "promotions from within," which benefit rank-and-file employees but do not always benefit the service.

The President, in seeking to balance the budget, is regularly confronted with the fact that it has cost approximately 1 billion dollars more to run the Post Office Department each year than were collected in postal receipts. Yet, whenever the President proposes an increase in postal rates, the Congress is reluctant to vote for his proposals because of the vigorous opposition of newspaper and magazine publishers, direct-mail advertisers, and others. Business interests that use the service extensively are, in effect, subsidized by low postal rates.

[4] For a more extended discussion of civil rights, see C. Herman Pritchett, *The American Constitution* (McGraw-Hill Book Company, Inc., New York, 1959), part 6, "First Amendment Freedoms."

Many other businesses are similarly subsidized (e.g., trucking, merchant marine, and air transport) by the provision of other governmental services. The repeated question is: Are the functions performed by these businesses—the publishers and the advertisers—of such good to the public interest as to warrant a subsidy of more than 1 billion dollars a year paid by all taxpayers?

PROMOTION AND THE PUBLIC INTEREST

The major function of five executive departments is to "promote" the interests of particular groups. The central problem involved in the administration of each is: How shall the condition of the particular group (e.g., farmers) be bettered while still protecting the general interests of the whole citizenry of the United States?

THE DEPARTMENT OF AGRICULTURE This department faces a dilemma. The committees on agriculture of the Senate and of the House of Representatives and the farm organizations[5] hold the Department responsible for the welfare of the millions of people who live and work on this country's farms. The Congress appropriates over 5 billion dollars annually so that the Department, with its 90,000 employees, can discharge this responsibility. Three-fourths of this expenditure goes into programs designed to maintain farm prices and to stabilize farmers' incomes. Yet this country's needs for food and fiber could be supplied by many fewer farmers cultivating fewer acres of land.

The Assistant Secretary, who is in the "middle of things" most of the time, supervises the work of the Commodity Credit Corporation, the Commodity Stabilization Service, and the Federal Crop Insurance Corporation. Through these agencies he supervises the price-support programs for corn, wheat, tobacco, cotton, and other crops. Secondly, he supervises the acreage allotment programs, which are designed to bring the production of certain crops into line with the demand for these crops. Thirdly, he is responsible for insuring the farmers' investments in the production of crops against loss from causes beyond their control, such as weather, insects, and disease.

Other less controversial activities are designed to make our farms more efficient and productive. These are carried on in collaboration with the state governments and are supervised by the Assistant Secretary for Federal-States Relations. For example, the Agricultural

[5] Among the largest and most powerful are the American Farm Bureau, the National Grange, and the Farmers Union.

Research Service laboratories carry on research in the production and utilization of agricultural products. The Federal Extension Service carries the result of such research to the farmers through the land grant colleges and their extension services in each state and through the county agents. The Forest Service, and its distinctively able career service, administers 154 national forests, including more than 180 million acres of land, works with the states and private forest land owners in cultivating these forests, and carries on extensive research in nine experiment stations.

Still other programs and units provide farmers with credit. The Farmers Home Administration makes loans to aid tenants, laborers, and sharecroppers own farms, to enable farmers to improve their lands, to help local organizations to improve watersheds and farmers to construct or improve buildings. The Rural Electrification Administration makes loans to public bodies and cooperatives to bring electricity and telephone service to farm homes.

The Department's Economics Research Service carries on continuing studies to determine how our agricultural industry can be adjusted to an era of abundance. The Foreign Marketing Service helps the adjustment by planning the distribution of surplus crops to foreign countries as a form of aid. And other units within the Department strive in other ways to shrink what was this country's major industry to modern needs.

The complexity of the Secretary of Agriculture's job grows out of the necessity of "promoting" the prosperity of farm people while furthering the essential adjustment of agriculture to the needs of the current American society. The discharge of these responsibilities requires political courage as well as wisdom.

THE DEPARTMENT OF COMMERCE This department is responsible for fostering, promoting, and developing the country's foreign and domestic commerce and its manufacturing, shipping, and transportation industries. The Secretary of Commerce speaks for the most powerful economic interests in the country. Despite his powerful clientele, no Secretary of Commerce has ever been a powerful figure, either within the Federal government or with the business interests he is expected to represent. The explanation of this anomaly is twofold. First, business is divided: if the Secretary pleases big business, he is likely to antagonize small business; if he pleases domestic producers, he may irk importers. Secondly, the Department provides few services that directly benefit individual businesses as stabilization payments benefit farmers.

The Business and Defense Services Administration, Census Bureau, and the Office of Business Economics of the Department assemble and distribute information of general value to businessmen and others (e.g., the farmers) alike. The Bureau of Foreign Commerce, the Office of International Trade Affairs, and the Advisory Committee on Export Policy of the Department encourage trade between American and foreign businessmen. The National Bureau of Standards and the Coast and Geodetic Survey provide scientific information of value to businessmen, and the Patent Office protects inventions by the issuance of patents.

Two-thirds of the Department's annual budget is expended under the guidance of an Under Secretary for Transportation, who supervises a number of activities that are of value to business. The Bureau of Public Roads administers large grants to state governments for the building of a national system of highways. The Weather Bureau similarly provides information of value to the aircraft, agricultural, and other industries and to the population generally. The only large subsidy administered by the Department is that for the merchant shipping industry, which receives subsidy payments of approximately 300 million dollars annually distributed by the Maritime Administration.

Comparisons between the Department of Commerce and the Department of Agriculture point up certain differences. Approximately 60,000 men and women are employed in the Department of Commerce, as compared with 90,000 in the Department of Agriculture. The Department of Commerce expends less than 50 million dollars annually for research, a sum considerably smaller than the 150 million dollars or more spent by the Department of Agriculture. Most of the research and development that is of interest to business is done or contracted for by the Atomic Energy Commission, the Department of Defense, and the National Aeronautics and Space Administration.

The Department of Commerce does not administer large-scale credit operations for the benefit of businessmen similar to those administered by the Farm Credit Administration and REA in the Department of Agriculture for the benefit of farmers. The principal Federal agencies which extend credit to business firms—the Housing and Home Finance Agency and the Small Business Administration—are not part of the Department of Commerce. Yet, more than 50 million men and women are employed by the business firms that make up the clientele of the Department of Commerce, while 6 million men and women are employed on this country's farms. These contrasts demonstrate the strong political influence of farmers. They illustrate the difficulties of the job of the Secretary of Commerce.

THE DEPARTMENT OF THE INTERIOR   For two centuries this country has been blessed with plenty of natural resources. Now we must husband our public lands, our mineral resources, our sources of power, and our water if we are to have enough for a much larger population. It is the responsibility of the Department of the Interior to conserve, develop, and manage publicly owned mineral resources, land, and water, which are of infinite value.

Approximately 40 per cent of the total annual expenditure of this Department is for the management of public lands. This task—the fighting of fires on these lands, the building of access roads, the leasing of lands to graziers and others, and their maintenance as recreational areas—is the work of five bureaus. These are the Bureau of Land Management, the Bureau of Indian Affairs, the National Park Service, the Office of Territories, and the Alaska Railroad. The national forests, which constitute a substantial portion of this country's public lands, are administered by the U.S. Forest Service, a unit within the Department of Agriculture.

Conservation of this nation's mineral resources utilizes about a ninth of the Department's annual budget. The task includes the mapping and experimental work of the Geological Survey, the research and safety work of the Bureau of Mines, the development of new methods of mining and utilizing coal by the Office of Coal Research, and other activities designed to encourage exploration for minerals and to mobilize the resources we would need if war came.

An equal proportion of the Department's annual budget goes for conservation of fisheries and wildlife. This task includes research and other efforts to protect and build our fisheries and wildlife.

A sum approximately equal to that going each year for the management of public lands goes for water and power development. It is spent for the construction and maintenance of irrigation projects by the Bureau of Reclamation and the generation and transmission of power by the Bonneville, the Southeastern, and the Southwestern power administrations. In addition, during the early sixties the Department quadrupled its annual expenditure for the development of low-cost processes for converting salt water into fresh water—an urgent need in many foreign countries, as well as in parts of our own.

The great value of the natural resources in the Department's care makes it a natural target for large and powerful business interests, especially the mining, power, and petroleum industries. The Department's relationship to the pressure groups representing these and other industries is quite different from the relationship of the Department of Agriculture or the Department of Commerce to the pressure groups with which they work. In its efforts to preserve natural resources, the Department of the Interior often faces the vigorous opposition of pressure groups.

THE DEPARTMENT OF LABOR   Although it is one of the smallest of all executive departments, the relative solidarity and political strength of its constituency—especially organized labor—give it a significant influence in the formation of government policies. More than 60 per cent of the staff of the Department (about 62,000 persons) are employed in three units—the Bureau of Employment Security, the Bureau of Labor Statistics, and the Wage and Hour and Public Contracts Division.

These three units and eight others that make up the Department have a common objective: to protect workers and promote their welfare as wage earners, to improve their working conditions, and to advance their opportunities for profitable employment. The Secretary of Labor advises the President on issues and policies relating to labor, labor-management relations, and unemployment. In addition, he is frequently called upon to assist with the settlement of labor disputes. Under some Presidents the Secretary of Labor has been relied on to give general surveillance to the functioning of such independent agencies as the National Labor Relations Board and the Federal Mediation and Conciliation Service.

The Department is, of course, the focus of the attention of the major labor organizations—the AFL-CIO, the United Mine Workers, and others. But it is the agency of government concerned with the interests of unorganized as well as organized workers. Hence, in his dealings with the Senate and House committees on Labor and Education and in his direction of the Department, the Secretary (especially if he was once associated with organized labor) is likely to be criticized as being the mouthpiece of organized labor.

The Secretary of Agriculture is expected to speak for the farmers. The Secretary of Commerce is counted on to voice the views of business. But the realities of American economic and political life require that the Secretary of Labor not offend management, even while he is obligated to promote the interests of working people.

THE DEPARTMENT OF HEALTH, EDUCATION, AND WELFARE Abraham Ribicoff, when retiring as Secretary in 1962, commented that the management of the five major agencies—the Office of Education, the Food and Drug Administration, the United States Public Health Service, the Social Security Administration, and the Office of Vocational Rehabilitation—that make up this Department, is an impossible task. Their annual budgets approximate 3 billion dollars. The bulk of this sum is used to make grants to state governments; hence, the operational problem is how to persuade, cajole, and convince state officials to do what, in the opinion of Department officials, should be accomplished with these monies.

People, their congressmen, and state officials are interested in such matters as the prevention and care of heart disease and cancer; alleviation of the shortage of teachers; the availability of financial assistance to needy, aged persons, to the blind, and to dependent children; the provision of medical care for the aged; and assurance of the purity of the foods and drugs they buy. This interest stimulates the substantial and continuing pressure of such organizations as the American Public Welfare Association, the American Medical Association (usually an opponent of the Department), the Association of State and Territorial Health Officers, the National Education Association, the American Council on Education, and others. These strong pressure groups give to each of the Department's five major agencies independent political support, and this tends to make more difficult the Secretary's task of managing a Department composed of relatively independent units.

Ninety per cent of the Department's 64,000 employees are employed in two major units: the United States Public Health Service and the Bureau of Old Age and Survivors Insurance in the Social Security Administration. The first of these conducts a large variety of public health activities, especially research into the causes of illness and death. The latter, which has more than 500 offices throughout the country, administers the insurance program that provides benefits for retired workers, widows and orphans of deceased workers, and disabled workers.

The five departments that have been described as "promotional" departments regulate, even as they promote. The Department of Agriculture aids the farmer only as he conforms to stipulated requirements, for example, crop controls; the Department of Health, Education, and Welfare makes grants to the states only as they conform with criteria as to the use of such funds; the Department of Commerce through the Maritime Administration regulates the design, construction, and operation of United States ships on the high seas, even as it promotes our shipping industry.

ADMINISTRATION THROUGH INDEPENDENT AGENCIES

Thirty-five independent agencies (that is, agencies outside the executive departments whose heads report directly to the President) have been created since 1930. Each reflects the government's provision for another need of the country's population. Some of these agencies, such as the Selective Service System, were created for a temporary purpose and survived; others, such as the Veterans Administration, were created to provide for specific needs that they continue to serve.

The independent agency permits the President to focus administrative attention on a developing problem of public concern. For example, to give greater assurance of the safety and efficiency of our airways, the Federal Aviation Agency was created in 1959. The FAA is responsible for the administration of Federal aid to municipalities for building airports, for increasing the safety of air transport—for which it trains inspectors, licenses pilots, and carries on an extensive research program—and for the development of advanced aircraft, for example, the design and development of a supersonic transport. The FAA was created especially to develop a common system, with the Department of Defense, for operating the large number of traffic control towers and related air navigational facilities that guide both military and civilian aircraft.

The FAA faces a problem common to most Federal departments and agencies: it must seek to accomplish what it believes is in the public interest while "getting along with" powerful interest groups. These include the Aircraft Owners and Pilots Association, the Airline Pilots Association, the Air Transport Association, the Aircraft Industries Association, the Airport Operators Council, and the General Aviation Advisory Council.

The largest and oldest of the independent agencies is the Veterans Administration. It was created many years ago to look out for those who had served their country in the armed forces. In the sixties it employs a staff of more than 170,000 and expends more than 6 billion dollars annually in the payment of veterans' benefits (amounting to about 3 billion dollars annually), in the maintenance of an insurance program for veterans, and in the operation of hospitals, domiciliaries, and clinics which care for an average daily patient load of approximately 115,000.

President John F. Kennedy repeatedly urged, unsuccessfully during 1961 and 1962, that the Housing and Home Finance Agency be converted into an executive Department of Urban Affairs. His recommendation reflects the impact of urbanization on the Federal government—the need for a Federal agency to deal with the increasing variety of problems that confront this country's burgeoning metropolitan centers.

The Housing and Home Finance Agency resulted from the merger of several formerly independent agencies concerned with planning the redesign of our cities, stimulating the renewal of slum areas, developing transportation for suburbanites, and building housing for low-income families. It includes the Federal Housing Administration (FHA), Public Housing Administration (PHA), Urban Renewal Administration (URA), Office of Transportation, Community Facilities Administration (CFA), and the Federal National Mortgage Association ("Fannie Mae").

Another major independent agency, the Tennessee Valley Authority (TVA), was established in 1933 under the leadership of Franklin D. Roosevelt to develop the entire Tennessee Valley. It built its program around utilization of the waters of the Tennessee River and its tributaries, controlling these to prevent floods and using them for irrigation and for the generation of power. It has attracted the interest of public administrators throughout the world, and it has consistently attracted the criticism of opponents of Democratic administrations.

GOVERNMENT IN THE ADMINISTRATION OF SCIENCE

The Federal government has long studied ways of putting science to work for the American people. The Department of Agriculture, for example, has studied the use of soils, the control of pests, and other farm problems. The United States Public Health Service has studied the causes and cure of many diseases. The National Bureau of Standards has carried on research as to the development and use of uniform techniques of physical measurement. Since World War II, however, the Federal government's concern with science has grown enormously.

The Atomic Energy Commission was created in 1946 to provide for an awesome, mysterious, and highly dangerous weapons manufacturing process. From the start the AEC has operated a series of laboratories to develop this amazing new force and to apply it for the benefit of mankind. So that the country's best brains might be put to work on these problems, the AEC contracted with major universities (e.g., California and Chicago) and with private contractors to operate the laboratories. The Commission itself, a bipartisan group of five men, supervises a relatively small staff in Washington concerned with planning and contracting for the research needed.

The National Aeronautics and Space Administration was born of the surprise experienced in this country when the Russian Sputnik orbited the earth. This incident dramatically demonstrated the opportunities for exploration in space, and the Federal government responded by converting the older National Advisory Committee on Aeronautics into a new and substantial agency. This agency consists of a small staff of 850 scientists in Washington and more than 20,000 scientists, technicians, and others employed in seven major laboratories throughout the country. Each is engaged in planning space exploration or in developing boosters or craft which will fly beyond the atmosphere.

The National Science Foundation was created in 1950 to lead and stimulate the Federal government's participation in the field of science. It seeks to achieve this end by initiating and supporting basic scientific research, by awarding scholarships and fellowships, by making grants to the universities and to individuals engaged in science that promises general benefits to the American society, and by coordinating and evaluating scientific research by Federal agencies. The NSF employs approximately 900 men and women in divisions concerned with the biological and medical sciences, the mathematical and physical sciences, the social sciences, and scientific personnel and education. The director of the NSF is advised by a National Science Board made up of eminent scientists and men of affairs. He and his staff maintain continual communication with the scientists throughout the country, in part through the National Academy of Sciences and simultaneously through the several universities.

The creation of these agencies and the rapidly increasing impact of science on the work of the Department of Defense and other agencies resulted in the establishment, during President Eisenhower's tenure, of the President's Scientific Advisory Board and subsequently the appointment of a Scientific Adviser to the President. These steps preceded the establishment of the Office of Science and Technology in the Executive Office of the President, and it is clear in retrospect, that they were essential to enable those who head the Executive Branch —the President and his department heads—to ensure the efficient handling of the emerging problems of science and government.

RELATIONSHIP OF DEPARTMENTS AND AGENCIES TO CONGRESS

The executive departments and agencies have been seen as units of the organization which the President administers. Yet, it must be emphasized that those who "run" these units of the executive branch are responsible to the Congress as well as to the President. The heads of these units are appointed by the President, but they are also responsible to the Congress and to congressional committees, which exercise an important oversight of all executive branch activities.

To carry out his responsibilities successfully, the Secretary of Commerce must maintain cordial and cooperative relations with the House and Senate Appropriations Committees, the House and Senate Interstate and Foreign Commerce Committees, the House and Senate Public Works Committees, the House Merchant Marine and Fisheries Committee, the House Ways and Means Committee, and the Senate Government Operations Committee. Similarly, the Chairman of the Atomic Energy Commission works continually with the Joint Committee of the Congress on Atomic Energy. So it is with each department and agency. They serve the President well only when they can maintain the confidence and support of the relevant committees of Congress— those that enact the legislation and pass upon appropriations they need.

Outside the government these officials must work with the pressure groups that are interested in the department's activities. The active support of such groups is often necessary to secure congressional approval of advances in programs and adequate appropriations. The Veterans Administration, for example, is of prime concern to the American Legion and each organized veterans' group. The Department of Labor similarly must work with and maintain the confidence of the AFL-CIO, the United Mine Workers, and others. The Department of Health, Education, and Welfare must work with and have the support of certain groups, among them the organized "educational industry" (e.g., the National Education Association and the American Council on Education). Each official, in short, must possess that unique skill that enables him to communicate understanding of his activities to these interest groups and to maintain their support without becoming their "captive." He must be able to distinguish the clamor of special interest groups and of lobbies from the voice of the people.

Each secretary is aided in achieving this, and in the general management of his department, by two principal groups of assistants. The first group includes the under and assistant secretaries, who are appointed to make effective the policies of the party in power. In doing this they usually supervise certain bureaus or agencies of the department (e.g., the agencies concerned with water and power development in Interior) review and formulate policies, and represent the Department to the interest groups and to the Congress.

The second group of assistants consists of the top career civil servants as, for example, the Director of the Bureau of Prisons in the Department of Justice or the Chief Forester who heads the U.S. Forest Service in the Department of Agriculture. These men and women are experts and managers. They "run" the bureaus and offices that do much of the government's work. But they run these units in accordance with policies laid down by their political superiors—the secretary and the under and assistant secretaries.

PRESIDENTIAL LEADERSHIP

The competing interests of various demands (a dollar spent for national defense cannot be used to support public education) and the rivalry of strong pressure groups (e.g., the National Association of Manufacturers versus the AFL-CIO) make the Federal government a jungle of conflict rather than an "administration" devoted to achieving the goals stated during the previous campaign. The one force that can give direction to the efforts of the numerous departments and agencies is the leadership of the President.[6] And the power any President has is in direct proportion to the extent he grasps the power of this office—and leads.

[6] For a fuller discussion of presidential leadership, see Rowland Egger and Joseph P. Harris, *The President and Congress*, McGraw-Hill Book Company, Inc., New York, 1963, chaps. 1–3.

How does the President exercise leadership? Through the use of power over his political party? Yes, and this means continually building the strength of and his control over the party by such grubby work as raising funds at political dinners, influencing the selection of his party's candidates in strategic races, and building his party's organization in cities and states, as well as nationally, by consulting, often when time is scarce, with politicians of all ranks and factions in his party and, of course, by stump oratory.[7]

Does the President exercise leadership through use of the power the Constitution gives him as leader of the people? Yes, for on many issues on which he must lead (e.g., segregation) he must find support in both parties. Does he lead through the use of words? Yes, for in his public addresses and congressional messages he builds the public interest, understanding, and approval that is the raw material of his power.

But presidential leadership is all this and more; it is the President's capacity to gain and hold public support while he makes decisions that vitally affect many citizens and to see these decisions through, that is, to see that despite opposition by vested interests and partisan opponents his administration gets the results that he decides are desirable. No better illustration can be offered than President Kennedy's forceful persuasion of the steel companies to rescind an announced price increase in April, 1962.

The President's task in administration is one of supervising more than two hundred separate departments and agencies. But his administration of the Federal government is never limited to directing employees in the efficient conduct of specific activities. He must at the same time mobilize political and popular support. In the final analysis the public administrator—President or department or agency head— must earn and retain the confidence of citizens, their belief that the government is acting in their best interest.

Review Questions

1. The President of the United States is sometimes described as "the Chief Executive." When applied to the President

---

[7] See Tom Wicker, "'A Total Political Animal,'" *The New York Times Magazine*, Apr. 15, 1962, for informative description of the tactics of leadership of John F. Kennedy as President.

what does the term "executive" comprehend? In what ways would you expect the President's staff to differ from, let us say, the President of the General Motors Corporation?

2. Look up in the daily newspaper the record of the President's doings on a typical day. What do you visualize his appointments secretary, or one of his special assistants, had to do with each of the visitors or meetings the President participated in?

3. As a young staff member of the Bureau of the Budget (where the best-trained young students of public administration go to work in the Federal government) what kinds of tasks might you be engaged in?

4. What kinds of changes have taken place over recent decades in the administration of foreign affairs? What effect do you think these changes have on the kinds of men and women required in the Department of State and other agencies involved?

5. Consider the administration of the Department of the Treasury. What kind of experience, what breadth of understanding, or what skills would be required in the Secretary and his principal aides to comprehend and, hence, effectively supervise the work of the several bureaus and agencies that make up this department?

6. Can you list five legal problems, issues, or cases that attracted widespread public attention? In which of these would the Department of Justice be involved?

7. Why should the Federal government maintain large departments to promote the interests of special groups—farmers, business, and labor—within the total American society?

8. The Department of Health, Education, and Welfare is the most recently established executive department. Why, in your opinion, was a department concerned with these functions so late coming into being?

9. Why are independent agencies independent? In other words, what accounts for the existence of each of the major independent agencies outside of the executive departments and for their direct responsibility to the President?

10. Can you cite notable instances during recent years in which a President manifested special leadership? What do those instances indicate as to the means a President uses to lead the American people?

ADMINISTERING OUR NATIONAL DEFENSES

Chapter 5

SCOPE AND ENVIRONMENT

Before World War II, the Departments of War and Navy included less than 400,000 civilian and military personnel and operated on an annual budget of 900 million dollars. By 1962, after 17 years of restless peace following World War II, the Department of Defense, with its three subordinate departments—Army, Navy, and Air Force—employed 3.75 million civilian and military personnel in its regular establishment; its annual expenditures approached 53 billion dollars. By such measures the administrative job of the Department is vast; it is also unprecedented in complexity.

The job grows in size and complexity, first, because of the growing strength—in terms of population, economic resources, and technological capacity to build more destructive weapons—and the obviously aggressive intent of the enemy. The American people have been forced to realize that they can have peace only by making the leaders of the U.S.S.R. realize that we are strong. Second, the administrative job requires the continual replacement of present weapons (jet planes and tanks) with the most modern weapons that a rapidly evolving technology can produce (hydrogen bombs, space satellites, missiles, and supersonic bombers). Third, the administrative job can be planned effectively only if there is a continual flow of intelligence on a broad spectrum of matters ranging from logistics to factory location and design and the state of mind and health of peoples all over the globe. Fourth, the job involves this country's mobilization of the strength of all other nations devoted to the democratic idea. It necessitates to a greater degree than ever before the continual utilization of the vast productive power possessed by American industry.

The scope of the administrative job of the Department of Defense is enormous. Its accomplishment is made difficult also by the fact that day-to-day administration is inextricably related to or affected by all the political, economic, and scientific developments throughout the world. Think, for example, how the stability of governments in Iran, Laos, or Korea affects this country's defense program. Consider the relation of the rate of this country's economic growth to the rate of its military buildup. The effect of each of these and other factors must be considered in carrying out the administration of our defenses.

The Department's activities directly involve more than 8.5 million persons, including men and women in the regular forces and the reserves, and those employed by the Department as civilian workers. Indirectly the Department's activities affect from 8 to 10 million other persons who work for private employers, especially in the aircraft, missile, electronics, and related industries, under government contracts. Through contracts with industrial firms, universities, or others, the Department supports about a third of all current research and development in this country. Its activities, that is, its recruitment of men and women, its contracting for goods and services, and its efforts to protect civilians in the event of an attack, are apparent in every community throughout the nation, in 20 foreign countries where bases are maintained, and in those foreign countries where military assistance is provided.

THE ORGANIZATIONAL SETTING

The Constitution makes the President the Commander in Chief of our nation's military forces. But the Secretary of Defense administers this country's defenses. He is responsible for proposing to the President the kind of defense program our national security requires, for planning how more than half of the total Federal budget is to be spent each year to assure our national security, and for executing the vast program.

To accomplish his job, the Secretary of Defense must work with and through eight Federal agencies which form the major elements of this country's organizational "shield."

The *National Security Council* (see pages 56–57) was used less by President Kennedy at the start of his administration than it had been by his predecessor, but, after the failure of the Cuban invasion in 1961, it convened more regularly. At the time of the "Cuban crisis" in October, 1962, it was an executive committee of the NSC that met with the President daily and counseled him on successive steps to be taken. Essentially this group represented the departments through which the President carried out his policies.

The supersecret *Central Intelligence Agency* (see page 56), created in 1947 to coordinate all intelligence activities of the military services and to carry on a world-wide intelligence-gathering effort, is in daily contact with the Defense Intelligence Agency, the intelligence services of the military departments, and the National Security Agency.

The *Office of Emergency Planning* (see page 56) is responsible for planning the maintenance of this country's economy in the event of war. Its work brings it into regular contact with the Department of Defense. The relationship of the Department with this agency is of less consequence to the Department, however, than its relationship with other agencies that constitute the nation's organizational shield.

Work with the *Department of State* (see pages 59–60) has increased as the need for more effective coordination of diplomatic and military matters has become more apparent since World War II. Policies as to what we will stand for or do in Berlin, Cuba, or Vietnam involve decisions as to where we shall send troops, planes, and ships and establish missile bases; which countries we shall provide with military equipment and technical advice; which countries we shall provide with economic aid; as well as political and diplomatic actions.

Hence, the staffs of the Departments of Defense and State are inter-related by many formal and informal committees, liaison officers, and procedural devices. The Assistant Secretary (International Security Affairs) handles for the Secretary many of the relationships with the Department of State. He is responsible for matters that involve the United States Mission to the United Nations (e.g., an issue to be debated in the United Nations), the Agency for International Development (e.g., economic aid to be granted to countries whose military strength we are building), the United States Information Agency, the Export-Import Bank, and other "international" agencies.

The *Atomic Energy Commission* (see page 71) is intimately inter-related with the Department of Defense in the production of atomic bombs and in the development of such weapons as nuclear-powered submarines, aircraft carriers, and aircraft. A Military Liaison Committee chaired by the Assistant to the Secretary of Defense (Atomic Energy) provides a formal means for considering mutual problems. In addition, military personnel are assigned to the Commission to work on specific projects, and a myriad of day-to-day contacts exist between officials of the two agencies.

With increasing frequency in the years since 1960 questions have been raised in Congress and by the public as to whether the space exploration program carried on by the *National Aeronautics and Space Administration* (see page 71) handicaps the development of our military strength or whether military space programs wastefully overlap or impede civilian space exploration. These questions arise naturally from the fact that while NASA carries on an extensive research and production program (annual budget for fiscal year 1963, 3.8 billion dollars) to enable this country to explore outer space, the Department of Defense, particularly the department of the Air Force, builds missiles that can be used as weapons to deliver an atomic warhead on enemy territory or to propel a surveillance satellite into orbit to detect enemy installations.

The principal formal point for coordination between NASA and the Department of Defense is the National Aeronautics and Space Council. This body is headed by the Vice President and includes the Secretary of Defense, the Secretary of State, the Administrator of NASA, and the Chairman of the Atomic Energy Commission. In addition, NASA's staff is regularly in contact with Defense officials over scores of related matters; for example, when an astronaut is shot into space, the arrangements for tracking his flight and for ensuring his safe landing are the result of weeks of previous planning by NASA and Defense officials as to where ships and planes will be stationed and how overseas tracking stations will record the astronaut's whereabouts from minute to minute.

The efforts of the *Federal Aviation Agency* (see page 69) to develop an improved national air traffic control and navigation system for both military and civil aircraft and its planning and conduct of research on air navigation facilities bring it into continual contact with the Department of Defense. The work of the FAA and the Department of Defense is coordinated through an interagency committee, on which the Assistant Secretary of the Air Force (Material) is the principal Department of Defense representative, and through direct contact at lower levels in the Air Force and Navy.

In 1961, even while we were striving vigorously to build our armed strength, the Congress established the *United States Arms Control and Disarmament Agency* within the Department of State. This agency was created to conduct research, recommend policies, and carry on negotiations for international disarmament under the direction of the Secretary of State. To accomplish these tasks the Disarmament Agency must work with and coordinate activities of the Department of Defense, the AEC, NASA, and other government agencies.

THE ADMINISTRATIVE PROCESS WITHIN

THE SECRETARY'S AIDES Immediately under the Secretary is the civilian staff, which consists of the Deputy Secretary, the Director of Defense Research and Engineering, six assistant secretaries, the General Counsel, and assistants to the Secretary for legislative affairs and for atomic energy. Each is responsible for giving leadership and direction to a function and for formulating policies and supervising their execution throughout the Department. The accompanying figure shows the organization of the Department of Defense.

The Armed Forces Policy Council consists of the Secretary and Deputy Secretary of Defense, the secretaries of the three military departments, the Director of Defense Research and Engineering, the Chairman of the Joint Chiefs of Staff, and the chief of staff of each military department. The Commandant of the Marine Corps regularly attends the Council's meetings. The Council is the mechanism through

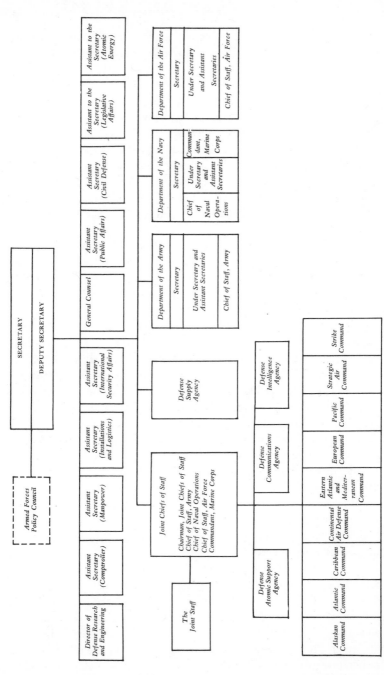

The Department of Defense.

which the Secretary confers with his top staff on all matters of broad policy and on the most important problems that confront the Department.

THE COMMAND LINES   Within the Department administrative authority flows from the Secretary through two lines of command. One, for the direction of the support activities (i.e., the mobilization, training, equipment, and continuing provision of supplies for the forces), flows through the secretaries of the military departments and, since 1961, the Defense Supply Agency (see page 88). The other, for the operational direction of the Armed Forces stationed throughout the world, flows through the Joint Chiefs of Staff to the commanders of unified and special commands.

The support command line.   The secretaries of the subordinate military departments (i.e., Air Force, Army, and Navy) serve as the Secretary's "general managers." These three military departments were the original operating agencies of the defense establishment; they are now primarily concerned with support.

As an increased number of specialized agencies have been established separately from the military departments to perform centrally activities once performed by these departments, the support command line has been essentially bifurcated. Agencies such as the Defense Atomic Support Agency, the Defense Communications Agency, and the Defense Intelligence Agency, which exist to support military operations, report to the Joint Chiefs. The Defense Supply Agency is, however, the principal illustration of this bifurcation. It was created in 1961 to procure and stock a large number of common use items for each of the three military departments. Since it reports directly to the Secretary, it constitutes a parallel support command line.

The operational command line.   The Joint Chiefs of Staff are the military advisers to the President as well as to the Secretary of Defense. This body also aids the Secretary in formulating policy and overseeing its execution. It is headed by the Chairman, who is appointed by the President upon recommendation of the Secretary of Defense, and must be confirmed by the Senate. He has a large military staff composed of officers supplied by the four military services, and therein has lain its weakness. Since the members serve their own services first and serve secondly as members of the Joint Chiefs of Staff, they have tended to "represent" and fight for the interest of their own services rather than plan the best way to build the national defenses. And the

Chairman of the Joint Chiefs has seldom been strong enough or willing to push through the plans in which he believed.

The commanders of the unified and specified commands direct the Department's operational, or fighting, forces in the field. These commands report to the Joint Chiefs and constitute a highly significant adaptation of the Department's organization to the fact that wars are no longer fought separately on land, on the sea, or in the air. The commander of each is an officer of general or flag rank selected by the Secretary of Defense with the advice of the Joint Chiefs of Staff. Each has within his command forces supplied by each of the military departments.

These two command lines, then, represent the adaptation of our defense establishment to the age of nuclear power, missiles, space exploration, and a continuing cold war. Through these command lines the Secretary of Defense performs seven tasks: (1) strategic planning, (2) mobilizing and training forces, (3) developing future weapons, (4) the task of military support, (5) utilizing the fighting forces, (6) mobilizing the free world, (7) defending the home front.

STRATEGIC PLANNING

The first step in this task is to anticipate the possible military threats of the next 10–15 years, and then to develop concepts of the forces, matériel, and employment best suited to counter the possible threats. This task—strategic planning—goes on continually. It is performed by the "plans" divisions of the military staffs of each of the three service departments. But wars cannot be fought separately by armies, navies, and air forces. Hence, increasingly the planning process is centralized in the offices of the Joint Chiefs of Staff.

This planning is for at least three different kinds of war: all-out nuclear attack; a succession of limited or "brush-fire" wars such as have been experienced in the Congo, in Lebanon, and in Vietnam; or indefinite continuance of the cold war. The extent to which our plans emphasize one of these forms of war over another markedly affects the role and size of each service and the weapons to be developed and procured.

For example, if the planners forecast that there is little threat of all-out nuclear war but that this country must be prepared to fight a succession of "brush-fire" wars by guerrilla tactics in various parts of the world over the next decade, the Army will probably be expanded and expenditures for large transport planes increased, while the Air Force Strategic Air Command will be maintained but not expanded. For such decisions the Secretary of Defense and his aides require the best intelligence, military advice, knowledge of technological advance, and economic understanding that their staffs can provide. On such decisions the fate of the American people rests.

MOBILIZING AND TRAINING FORCES

Since the Korean conflict (1952–1953) the role of the military departments essentially has become that of developing and providing trained and fully equipped individuals and military units for the unified commands that make up our fighting forces and supporting these commands in peace and war. These departments no longer have the prime responsibility for fighting wars, as they did through World War II; they mobilize, train, equip, and deliver to the unified commands the forces needed (see Table 2). The military departments and services also develop and provide the "doctrine" (military concepts and practices) used in combat and support operations.

The forces of these service departments are built up, in principal part, through the enlistment or draft of individuals into the "regular" military services and through ordering to active duty individuals and units of the Reserve Components. The Reserve Components include the Army National Guard of the United States, the Air National Guard of the United States, the Naval National Guard of the United States, the U.S. Army Reserve, the U.S. Air Force Reserve, and the U.S. Marine Corps Reserve. In time of emergency, the Coast Guard and its Reserve serve under the Navy. The Reserve Officers Training Corps (ROTC) of the Army, Navy, and Air Force are primary sources of commissioned officer personnel for the regular military services and for the Reserve Components.

The task of manpower management is planned and carried out under the leadership of the Assistant Secretary of Defense (Manpower). Each of the military service secretaries has an assistant for manpower management, and under the chief of each military staff there are military staff units concerned with manpower (in the Navy the Bureau of Personnel, or BUPERS, and the Office of Industrial Relations, OIR).

The requirement that every young man shall serve in the Armed Forces during an extended peace–cold war poses both philosophical and social problems of manpower management, over and above the

TABLE 2 SUMMARY OF COMPOSITION OF MAJOR ACTIVE ARMED FORCES

DESCRIPTION	ACTUAL June 30, 1961	ESTIMATE June 30, 1962	ESTIMATE June 30, 1963
Military personnel (in thousands):			
Army	858	1,081	960
Navy	627	666	665
Marine Corps	177	190	190
Air Force	820	888	869
Total, Department of Defense	2,482	2,825	2,684
Military forces:			
Army:			
Divisions	14	16	16
Armored cavalry regiments and combat commands	7	6	6
Brigades	2	1	3
Battle groups, infantry	8	9	10
Missile commands	4	3	3
Air defense antiaircraft battalions	77	65	63
Surface-to-surface missile battalions	24	30	33
Helicopter aircraft inventory—active	2,721	2,785	3,039
Fixed-wing aircraft inventory—active	2,843	2,818	2,855
Navy:			
Commissioned ships in fleet	(819)	(898)	(862)
Warships	375	395	383
Other	444	503	479
Attack carrier air groups	17	18	17
Carrier antisubmarine air groups	11	12	11
Patrol and warning squadrons	38	53	35
Marine divisions	3	3	3
Marine air wings	3	3	3
Aircraft inventory—active	8,793	9,297	8,950
Air Force:			
USAF combat wings	(88)	(98)	(86)
Strategic wings	37	37	33
Air defense wings	19	18	17
Tactical wings	32	43	36
USAF combat support flying forces	(119)	(132)	(122)
Air refueling squadrons	65	67	59
MATS air transport squadrons	21	30	26
Other specialized squadrons	33	35	37
Aircraft inventory—active	16,905	16,244	15,449

SOURCE: *The Budget of the United States Government, Fiscal Year Ending June 30, 1963*, p. 62, 1962.

operating problems of recruitment, training, promotion, and morale. The philosophical problem concerns the citizen's obligation to serve in the Armed Forces in peacetime as well as in war. The social problems arise out of the companion facts that in the 1960s most young men seek and require more years of education and marry at an earlier age than was customary in earlier decades.

The staffing of the Armed Forces by the recruitment or drafting of large numbers for from six months to five years and then the replacement of most of these men requires large expenditures for training. But worse, these practices simply have not made it possible to acquire and retain the technically trained men and officers each of the services requires. In 1962 a significant proportion of the positions in which both officers and enlisted men are needed were vacant in each of the military departments.

DEVELOPING FUTURE WEAPONS

Keeping ahead in a cold war in the last half of the twentieth century is in substantial part a technological problem. To deter a threatening enemy requires an intensive effort to develop more efficient weapons before he does. Hence, perhaps the most important decisions made within the Department pertain to what research should be supported.

These decisions involve not only what should be done within the laboratories of the Army, the Navy, the Air Force, and the AEC, but what should be done by private contractors, nonprofit agencies, universities, and industrial contractors. More than 4 billion dollars (of a total of 5.5 billion) is expended annually under contracts with private aircraft, missile, electronics, and many other firms to produce new weapons for the armed services.

Any research, engineering, or development carried out within the Army, Navy, Air Force, or such Department of Defense agencies as the Advanced Research Projects Agency, the Weapons Systems Evaluation Group, and the Defense Atomic Support Agency is done under the supervision of the Director of Research and Engineering. This supervision is exercised through principal civilian officials, usually assistant secretaries, each responsible for overseeing research and development activities in a military department.

The decisions of these research and development officials are complicated by two obvious facts. The first is that such activities are carried on to provide the fighting units—Army and Marine divisions, Navy fleets and submarine groups, and Air Force wings—with the

EMPHASIS IN RESEARCH AND DEVELOPMENT
IS HEAVIEST IN MISSILES, BUT WEIGHT
IS MOVING TOWARD ASTRONAUTICS

*Defense Department obligations for research,
development, testing, and evaluation*

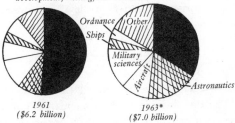

1961
($6.2 billion)

1963*
($7.0 billion)

Fiscal years

CHANGING TECHNOLOGY AND REEVALUATION
OF OUR MILITARY REQUIREMENTS BRING
SHIFTS IN PROCUREMENT

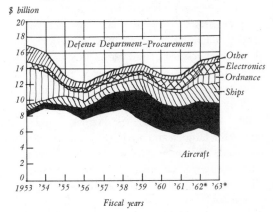

Fiscal years

*Estimate

(SOURCE: *Business in Brief,* The Chase Manhattan
Bank, March–April, 1962. DATA: *The Budget of the
U.S. Government, Fiscal Year Ending June 30, 1963;*
The Department of Defense.)

weapons and matériel needed; the research official must take into
account the realities of military use, as well as the technical factors
involved. The second is that these activities are inextricably related
to the support activities of each military service; that is, the research
official must determine whether the research and development is best
done within the Army's Matériel Command, the Navy's bureaus, or the

Air Force Logistics Command, or by outside contractors, and if by the latter, how the weapons, equipment, or supplies shall be procured and from what firm.

Conduct of these operations involves a continuing struggle between the scientist who strives to develop new and unprecedented weapons and the military officer who is accustomed to the proven weapons of the past. The officer's attitude has been popularly described as the "battleship mentality," for naval officers persisted in the desire to develop battleships after the advance of aircraft and the Polaris submarine had markedly limited the battleship's utility in today's wars. The same attitude of Army and Air Force officers has also delayed research and development decisions in those services.

THE TASK OF MILITARY SUPPORT

Consider the volume of food, petroleum, weapons, and a vast variety of other materials that must be transported halfway around the world to support the divisions, fleets, squadrons, and air wings that make up this country's Armed Forces. Consider, too, the task of constructing and maintaining the posts, camps, stations, shipyards, air bases, missile bases, and research laboratories needed throughout the world. Supplying these needs as well as many that are less easily recognized is a major administrative task of the Department of Defense.

Ten per cent of all the goods and services produced in the United States is consumed by the Armed Forces. Responsibility for seeing that this large segment of our economic resources is used efficiently is fixed, in principal part, on two Department of Defense officials: the Assistant Secretary (Financial Management) and the Assistant Secretary (Installations and Logistics). The former supervises the preparation of budgets and sees to it that efficient accounting, reporting, and internal audit processes are followed. The latter oversees the work of each of the military departments (through assistant secretaries for logistics in each) in planning the matériel they require, in production planning and scheduling, in procurement, in storing and distributing and managing inventories, and in many related activities.

The Assistant Secretary (Installations and Logistics) also supervises the agencies that perform support functions centrally, especially the Defense Supply Agency. This agency buys, stocks, and distributes commodities required by all three military departments, for example, petroleum, clothing, construction materials, photographic equipment, and medical supplies. Heretofore, an item such as petroleum might

have been purchased by the Army for distribution to all three departments. Now the petroleum products required by all departments are
bought by the Defense Supply Agency. Each military department still
maintains its own supply and logistics branch for those commodities
not handled by DSA.

The large annual expenditure for defense (much of which goes for
support) substantially influences our national economy and the profit-
ability of many large business enterprises, particularly in the aircraft
manufacturing, electronics, missile making, and shipbuilding industries.
Added expenditures for the purchase of military equipment mean more
jobs for workers, more profits for their employers, and more money
spent in the stores of those cities where "defense industry" is centered
(e.g., southern California). But added expenditures for defense may
bring inflation, and rising prices may harm many in the community.
To finance such increased defense expenditures requires high taxes.
These may curb inflation but add a heavy burden to citizens and
businesses alike.

The consequence is numerous "unholy alliances" between the military forces that earnestly desire more, bigger, and better weapons
and the congressmen in whose districts the industrial firms (and their
employee-voters) are located. Together they bring pressure upon
Department of Defense officials to decide upon the weapons they
favor and upon Congress to appropriate funds for such weapons.
Such pressures to build the B-70 aircraft in 1962 made the Secretary
of Defense's decision extremely difficult, provoked a critical dispute
between the executive branch and the Congress, and probably caused
the wasteful appropriation of funds.

UTILIZING THE FIGHTING FORCES

Although military leaders in each service reluctantly accepted the
obsolescence of separate ground, sea, and air warfare, they still clung
tenaciously to the maintenance of "command" authority over their
separate forces. But in 1958, when the Department was reorganized,
they were formally stripped of command authority. This action represented the final step in a long struggle between the forces of bureaucratic inertia and interservice jealousy, and those officials who saw
the necessity of adapting our military organization to the realities of
modern warfare.

The actual utilization of this country's fighting forces is entrusted
to nine commands; indeed, it can be said that the entire defense

organization exists to make these commands effective. Seven are made up of units—regiments, wings, and fleets—drawn from each of the military departments, and are headed by a commander responsible to the Secretary through the Joint Chiefs of Staff. These are the European, Caribbean, Pacific, Atlantic, Alaskan, Continental Air Defense, and the Strike commands. Two commands—the Strategic Air Command and the Eastern Atlantic and Mediterranean Command—are each composed of forces from a single service. The former is manned and led by the Air Force, the latter by the Navy.

The essential job of "supporting" each command—providing the continued flow of men and units, of matériel, from food to weapons, and of services (e.g., communications)—remains with the military departments. The practice has been that the department that supplies the commander will provide needed support.

MOBILIZING THE FREE WORLD

Our national security, many Americans have come to agree, depends not alone upon our own strength, but on the mobilization of the strength of all nations that believe as we do about the freedom of the individual. Hence, the Department of Defense provides military assistance to countries throughout the world so that they may better withstand aggression and combat internal subversion. Those who object to this activity contend that the governments of many countries we aid are unstable, that their countries are so small or weak as to be unable, no matter what we do for them, to oppose a strong enemy, and that much of our aid is wasted.

During the early sixties the cost of such assistance approximated 1.6 billion dollars each year. The Assistant Secretary (International Security Affairs) supervises the distribution of this military assistance to more than 40 countries. These include our allies in the North Atlantic Treaty Organization (NATO), our allies in the Southeast Asia Treaty Organization (SEATO), and lesser-developed countries on each continent. The more advanced countries are aided by our selling to them modern weapons and equipment. Some countries are aided by our providing more modern weapons and equipment and Military Assistance Advisory Groups (MAAGS) to train their forces. These groups are made up of senior military officers who work with the country's own military staffs, with the American Ambassador in the country, and with the relevant Unified Commander. Their plans

RIO TREATY			NATO	
Nations pledge themselves, in the event of aggression, to provide assistance on request. Members are:			*Members agree to regard an attack on one as an attack on all. Members are:*	
United States	Haiti	Peru	United States	Belgium
Cuba	Dominican Republic	Bolivia	Canada	Luxembourg
Honduras	Costa Rica	Paraguay	Iceland	Italy
Mexico	Panama	Brazil	Norway	Portugal
Guatemala	Venezuela	Chile	United Kingdom	France
El Salvador	Ecuador	Argentina	Netherlands	Greece
Nicaragua	Colombia	Uruguay	Denmark	Turkey
			W. Germany	
ANZUS TREATY			**SEATO**	
Members acknowledge that an attack in the Pacific against any will involve all. Members are:			*In case of aggression members are to "consult immediately in order to agree to measures which should be taken for common defense." Members are:*	
	United States		United States	New Zealand
	New Zealand		United Kingdom	Australia
	Australia		France	Philippines
			Pakistan	Thailand

CENTO
The U.S. is not directly a member of CENTO but has pledged to cooperate in mutual defense. Members are:
United Kingdom
Turkey
Pakistan
Iran

Military commitments of the United States around the world.

must be coordinated with the plans for economic assistance (in popular terms, "foreign aid") being provided to the same countries through the Agency for International Development of the Department of State.

The administrative responsibility of the military departments is threefold. First, they train the military officers they assign to individual countries to aid in the formulation of plans and in training forces. Second, they supply and deliver large quantities of fighting equipment. Third, they strive to standardize items of equipment in order to reduce the complexity of supply and to reduce costs, and they coordinate research and development efforts among our allies and ourselves.

DEFENDING THE HOME FRONT

In each war in this century, the American continent has been protected by the oceans which separate us on the East and West from potential enemies. Modern weapons of warfare have made obsolete these bodies of water as protectors of our population. The next war this country is forced to engage in will be the first war in which the American homeland is exposed.

In 1961 President Kennedy transferred the responsibility for the protection of civilians, especially against nuclear attack, from what was then known as the "Office of Civil and Defense Mobilization" to the Department of Defense. A new office was created at the assistant secretary level to formulate policies and administer our civil defense. The task involves the general supervision of Air Force agencies responsible for warning and of Army agencies responsible for the support of civilian governments and for the leadership of state directors of civil defense (appointed by the governors) and similar officials in many cities. For the first time the Department of Defense assumed responsibility for a governmental activity that it can conduct only by the leadership, the financial aid, and the stimulation of the state and local governments—a responsibility for which it was ill-prepared.

This responsibility includes all preparations that would protect (insofar as that is possible) civilians against a nuclear attack. This means the building of shelters; the training of civilians to detect fallout; and especially the training of local government officials (the chiefs of police, fire chiefs, public health directors, and others) to minimize casualties, restore living conditions, and maintain law and order if this country is attacked.

In major part the administration of our civil defenses, in the event of a nuclear attack by missiles, rests with the local governments. But the Department of Defense has been assigned responsibility for sounding the alarm in every local community (and perhaps every home) in the event of an attack, and, in advance, of ensuring that officials in every local community are trained and prepared to provide all those services that will protect citizens, and for ensuring that military forces will be available and trained to support local officials if their help is required.

In the early sixties civil defense protection concentrated on the building of shelters against radioactive fallout. It was assumed that if H-bombs were to strike our major cities, no one would survive in those areas, but that shelters might enable citizens in peripheral areas to survive. The proposal that shelters be built provoked many moral as well as economic arguments. Would our citizens be justified in building shelters for their protection if their allies abroad could not be expected to survive? Would life be worthwhile if Americans came out of the shelters to a country in which half or more of the livestock, foodstuffs, and other necessities had been destroyed? And would Americans be justified in expending perhaps 25 billion dollars for shelters when we might better stand the risk and spend this sum for schools?

THE NEED FOR PUBLIC SUPPORT

To accomplish any one of the foregoing seven tasks, the Secretary of Defense requires not only the assistance of able men as assistant secretaries and heads of departments, but the understanding and support of members of Congress as well. As a foundation for congressional support, he must have a favorable public opinion. To be effective in this job he must not only direct and supervise a massive organization capably but he must interpret the Department's plans and progress and continually build popular and political support for the defense program.

His success depends in large part on his ability and that of his colleagues to interpret the Department's plans and programs to congressional committees. The two major committees of the Congress with which he deals are the Armed Services Committees of the House of Representatives and the Senate. These committees are made up, in principal part, of congressmen who after years of service have become intimately familiar with operations of the Department. They expect and demand that they be consulted, and their experience is often more extensive than that of the Secretary. In addition, the Secretary and his aides regularly deal with the appropriations committees and other committees of both houses. Their success in persuading these committees determines in substantial part the course of our defense program.

Their success in persuading the Congress rests on the prevailing opinions of American voters and taxpayers. Some, however, argue that the present large appropriations have been gained by a "politics of anxiety," that is, by the persistent effort of Department of Defense civilian and military officials, industrialists, and congressmen to scare voters by overstating the prospect of attack. The persuasiveness of the Department of Defense is founded as well on the impact of the Department's decisions on every city, town, and family, and on many strong pressure groups, e.g., defense contractors, veterans, and reserve officers. The letting or cutback of a contract providing employment in a particular city, the activating or closing of a military camp or post, the extension of the draft or the calling up of reserves—these and many other actions of the Department influence public opinion of the defense program. Hence, the Secretary, with the aid of the Assistant to the Secretary (Legislative Relations) and the Assistant Secretary (Public Affairs); the secretaries of the military departments; and other interested officials, continually speak to, meet with, and cultivate the support of organized groups (the National Security Industrial Association, the American Legion, the American Bar Association, and others) concerned with the Department's actions.

AN EVOLVING FRAMEWORK

The organization of the Department of Defense is the result of a continual process of evolution since 1947. In that year the National Security Act created the "National Defense Establishment," headed by the Secretary of Defense, who was charged with the coordination of the three separate military departments that had grown large, strong, and important during World War II. His powers, which were limited to the formulation of general policies and to delicate persuasion, proved to be inadequate. As the years passed the magnitude and gravity of the national security problem became apparent, and led to successive reorganizations in 1949, 1953, 1958, and 1961. Each reorganization in turn brought increasing power to the center.

The Secretary of Defense has been granted more and more authority to control and direct (as distinguished from coordinate) the affairs of each department. The Chairman of the Joint Chiefs of Staff has been given increased authority to command the fighting forces, now organized in commands independent of the military departments. An increasing number of agencies (Defense Intelligence Agency, Defense Communications Agency, Defense Supply Agency, and Defense Electronics Agency) have been organized to perform centrally activities once performed separately in each military department. In short, the task of administering this country's national defense has been increasingly centralized. By 1963 this trend had attracted vigorous critics and opponents in the military services and in Congress.

A major step toward establishing the power of the Secretary of Defense was taken in 1961 when a new type of defense budget was presented to the Congress. It set forth the estimate of funds needed

TABLE 3 HOW THE MAJOR MILITARY PROGRAMS ARE GROUPED IN THE DEFENSE DEPARTMENT BUDGET

Each program covers the total funds for financing, including personnel, operation and maintenance, construction, procurement, and research. Obligational availability planned for fiscal 1963 is compared with the 1962 budget as amended.

MILITARY PROGRAM	OBLIGATIONAL AUTHORITY (BILLIONS OF DOLLARS)		SHARE OF 1963 AUTHORITY (per cent)		
	1962	1963	Procurement	R. & D.	Other
Strategic retaliatory forces Manned bombers, their tankers and air-launched missiles; intercontinental ballistic missiles (Atlas, Titan); Polaris submarines and their missiles and other elements of our central offensive forces	9.5	9.4	54	13	33
Continental air and missile defense forces Defense against airborne attack—e.g., manned interceptors, surface-to-air missiles (Nike-Hercules), surveillance and warning systems (DEW-line, BMEWS, SAGE)	2.2	2.1	27	1	72
General purpose forces Forces for use in general war or rapid deployment to any point in the globe in a limited military conflict. Contains a large proportion of conventional weaponry	18.2	18.4	51	1	48
Sealift and airlift forces Military Sea Transportation Service, Military Air Transportation Service, and Troop Carrier Wings of the Air Force.	1.1	1.3	55	5	40
Reserve forces Reserve components of the Army, Navy, Air Force, and Marine Corps. Planned strength—973,500 men at the end of fiscal 1963	1.8	1.9	14		86
Research and development All research, development, test, and evaluation not included in other programs—e.g., basic and applied research, space projects, B-70 prototype, antimissile missiles	4.7	5.7	2	90	8
General support Support activities of each service and agencies serving the entire Department of Defense—e.g., Defense Supply Agency, Defense Communications Agency, Defense Atomic Support Agency	12.1	12.8	15	4	81
Total Department of Defense—military functions (includes Civil Defense, not listed separately)	49.6	52.4	34	14	52

SOURCE: *Business in Brief*, The Chase Manhattan Bank, March–April, 1962.   DATA: The Department of Defense.

in terms of the basic military mission to be performed rather than, as traditionally, in terms of funds needed by each organizational sub-division, i.e., Army, Navy, or Air Force (see Table 3). The new type of budget accomplishes three things: (1) It brings together expenditures for programs that are expected to do the same kind of defense job (e.g., the Navy's Polaris and the Air Force's strategic bomber and missile programs, providing strategic retaliatory forces); (2) it brings together related costs, for example, in showing the costs of the Minuteman missile it added up the estimates of funds required for the missiles and for the personnel, operation, maintenance, construction, and research required to use the missile; and (3) it gives the Secretary of Defense more effective information with which to administer the Department.

THE STATUS OF CIVILIAN CONTROL

Since 1947, the traditional separation of civilian and military control over military matters has tended to disappear. For more than a century American tradition has held that while there should be ultimate civilian control of our military forces, the military staffs should be left free to make essential decisions as to military strategy and tactics. The technological evolution of warfare, the intermeshing of our defense program, and the carrying out of our foreign policy have tended to obliterate this traditional separation. The greatly increased power of the Secretary of Defense has raised criticisms that military leaders are "muzzled," that they are not free to advise the Congress and the people on military problems, and that congressional power to supervise the Armed Forces (in the words of the Constitution "to make rules for the government of the land and naval forces") is diminished.

Our country urgently needs professional military officers who are trained not only in military affairs but educated to understand this generation's social, economic, and political problems. Such officers should not, and have not, been muzzled in presenting informed views on these problems.[1] They have been, and should be, denied the opportunity to present partisan political views publicly or to the men they command. The voicing of partisan views publicly (not to the men of the armed services) is the responsibility of the politically designated

---

[1] See, for excellent discussion of this reasoning, William J. Thompson, Brigadier General (Ret.), U.S. Army, "Muzzle on the Military Mind," *Army*, vol. 12, no. 7, pp. 32–37, February, 1962.

head of the Department. And in today's world, he must be head in fact, if he is to utilize well the men and the money this country is putting to work on defense.

SPECIAL NONPROFIT CORPORATIONS

One further and still relatively novel institutional arrangement used by the Secretary of Defense and the secretaries of the military departments deserves mention. It is the nonprofit corporation created to perform specialized services under contract to the Department.

The oldest (established in 1947) and the best-known of the nonprofit agencies is RAND. It has been described as the "think factory for the Air Force." More exactly, it is an agency employing less than a thousand highly skilled economists, scientists, mathematicians, and engineers to perform a wide variety of analytical studies for the Air Force. In addition to RAND, the Air Force uses MITRE to conduct a series of studies and to oversee the efforts of a number of private contractors engaged in the building of our air defenses and Aerospace Corporation to plan and oversee the ballistic missile research and production program.

The Department of Defense contracted with the Institute for Defense Analyses to conduct a wide variety of analyses to aid the Secretary in decision making. Later, in October, 1961, it established the Logistics Management Institute. This independent nonprofit agency assembles highly talented business management specialists who study how the Department determines what to buy, the methods by which it buys, and how it manages its vast inventories. The department of the Army supports a similar nonprofit fact-finding agency known as the Research Analysis Corporation. The department of the Navy contracts for similar services with the Applied Physics Laboratory managed by the Johns Hopkins University.

More than a decade's experience demonstrates that these agencies have constituted a valuable administrative adjunct. They have been able to employ highly competent personnel, many of whom could not be recruited for work within the government. They have been able to maintain a nonbureaucratic, flexible environment in which competent, trained men and women could do creative work. They have manifested an independence of the departmental staffs, an ability to challenge constructively concepts and directions which subordinate officials within the departments cannot or will not do.

Yet the use of these "nonprofits" has been sharply challenged. Spokesmen in Congress criticize these agencies on the grounds that they pay "exorbitant" salaries, that they perform work that should be done only by employees within the government, and that they had been created to avoid the supervision of the Congress. Their future, and the substantial aid they had provided, is uncertain.

Of all men and women employed by government—Federal, state, and local—in the United States, one of every three is employed by the Department of Defense. The prospect of release from the dreadful threat of war and of relief from the heavy burden of building ever-larger defenses seems dim indeed. If the cold war continues for generations, this country's resources will be continually consumed in ensuring our national security, and the number of government employees in the Department will grow. Hence, the student of public administration must give special attention to the tasks, the structure, and the particular problems of defense administration.

Review Questions

1. How does the task of administering this country's defenses differ from what it was during World War II?

2. In what ways is the administration of the defense program related to or affected by other social, economic, or scientific developments within this country? Illustrate.

3. What are the lines of command within the Department of Defense?

4. In the administration of the Department of Defense, what are the principal jobs of the departments of Army, Air Force, and Navy and of the civilian secretaries that head these departments?

5. What is the role of "command" and through whom do the commanders report?

6. What is the technological problem that makes up a significant part of the administrative job of this country's defense job officials?

7. Why was responsibility for civil defense transferred to the Department of Defense?

8. Since the Department of Defense was created in 1947, what principal trends have marked its development?

9. What is the nature and what is the role of non-profit agencies in getting this country's defense job done? Illustrate.

10. Why does an "unholy alliance" between military leaders, industrialists, and members of Congress exist? Is it accurately described as "unholy" and why?

THE FEDERAL GOVERNMENT AND THE ECONOMY

Chapter 6

It is the extent and positive character of government's participation in the economy that distinguishes the administration of the Federal government in the second half of the twentieth century from that in earlier times. By taxing and spending, by making loans or granting subsidies to individuals and businesses, by paying benefits to the aged, the unemployed, and others, and by controlling the supply of money and credit, the Federal government not only stabilizes the American economy but, as one sage observer has written, furnishes "a growing share of the motive power that keeps the economy moving."[1]

Some contend that government cannot increase the total demand for goods and services and thus cannot produce economic growth. They contend that reducing what consumers spend (through taxing their money away) and increasing what government spends does not cause growth. To assess this argument consider the factors that determine the total volume of goods and services produced.

> The basic determinants of a society's productive capacity in any year [the Council of Economic Advisers has declared] are as follows:
>
> 1. The number of people available for employment, the number of hours they wish to work, their incentives and motivations, and their health, general education, occupational desires, and vocational skills;
>
> 2. The stock of new and old plant and equipment, and its composition by age, type, and location;
>
> 3. The terms on which the economy has access to natural resources, whether through domestic production or imports;
>
> 4. The level of technology, covering the range from managerial and organizational competence to scientific, engineering, and mechanical understanding;
>
> 5. The efficiency with which resources, domestic and foreign, are allocated to different economic ends, and the extent of monopolistic or other barriers to the movement of labor and capital from low-productivity to high-productivity uses.[2]

Activities of the Federal government can and do affect each of these factors. The control of immigration, for example, affects the number of people available for employment. The mediation of labor disputes, the training of workers, the financing of educatio~ ~~ ~~~ creation of employment for otherwise unemployed wo

[1] Alvin Hansen, *The New York Times Sunday Magazine*, Mar.
[2] *The Annual Report of the Council of Economic Advisers*, Ja
p. 111.

productivity. The taxing of businesses, paying subsidies to some, lending money to others, or contracting with still others influence their investment in plant, equipment, and inventories. Government controls over the importation or domestic production of oil or the importation of scarce minerals (cobalt, for example) influence how some industries grow and the prices of their products. Government support for scientific research constitutes still another important influence. And by loans, subsidies, benefits, spending, or taxes, government can (and does) "allocate" demand in such a way as to develop some industries—often the less-productive industries—rather than others.

CONTROLLING MONEY AND CREDIT

Government has long striven to level ups and downs in the economy by the use of monetary and credit controls. In the past the banks made the economy unstable by making loans and thus creating excessive spending power in periods of boom and by calling in loans and thus curtailing purchasing power when business conditions worsened. Thus, they aggravated the severity of cycles in business.

The Federal Reserve System was created to influence the actions of the banks by exercising controls over money and credit. The System is not an agency of the Federal Government; it is an independent agency owned by, and created to supervise the activities of, the commercial banks of this country. It has been described as a pyramid with a private base, a mixed middle, and a public apex.[3] The base is made up of quasi-public institutions (Federal Reserve banks) owned by private, national, and state-chartered banks. At the apex is the Board of Governors made up of seven members appointed by the President with the consent of the Senate. In the middle is the Open Market Committee composed of all seven Board members plus five of the twelve Federal Reserve bank presidents.

The Federal Reserve System uses four principal tools to influence the actions of the banks.

The first tool is the authority to change the rate of interest that the Federal Reserve Bank charges the commercial bank that wants to borrow money, i.e., the rediscount rate. This makes credit either more or less costly for the businessman. If the rate is raised, borrowers tend to ask for fewer loans; if it is lowered, to seek more loans.

The second tool is the power to set the legal ratio of bank reserves

[3] Michael Reagan, "Political Structure of the Federal Reserve," *The American Political Science Review*, vol. LV, no. 1, p. 64, March, 1961.

to deposits. By raising or lowering reserve requirements, it reduces or increases the funds the banks have to loan. Thus, it tightens or eases credit expansion.

Thirdly, it has authority to stipulate the minimum down payment in the purchase of common stocks. In times of war emergency this regulation has been applied to the purchase of such items as automobiles, refrigerators, ranges, and other goods.

Fourthly, it is authorized to sell or buy government securities, that is, to engage in open market operations. By selling government securities on the open market, the Federal Reserve Board can reduce total bank reserves. A lower reserve reduces the volume of deposits that the commercial banks can have. Conversely, if the Federal Reserve Board buys government securities in the open market the Federal Reserve banks give their checks to the buyers. These checks are deposited by commercial banks in their reserve accounts at a Federal Reserve bank and provide the additional reserve against which they can make more commercial loans.

These tools, plus the opportunity the Federal Reserve Board has to make suggestions to bankers, give it a large influence over the economy. Hence, it has often been contended that the System should be subject to greater control by the President. The national Commission on Money and Credit, for example, recommended in 1961, after a two-year study, that the Chairman and Vice Chairman of the Federal Reserve Board should be designated by the President from among the Board's membership, to serve a four-year term coterminous with the term of the President of the United States.[4] This step would make the Board mindful of the policies of the administration in power. It would enable the President (elected by the people) to have greater influence over how and when these tools are used.

THE LENDING PROCESS

At least 25 departments and agencies of the Federal government provide credit, in one way or another, to designated borrowers. Since World War II the volume of credit they have extended has grown tremendously. The purpose of these lending operations is to provide an adequate amount of credit at low interest rates in those fields where, for one reason or another, credit is not adequate or rates are high;

[4] *Money and Credit, Their Influence on Jobs, Prices, and Growth.* Report of the Commission on Money and Credit, Prentice-Hall, Inc., Englewood Cliffs, N.J., 1961.

TABLE 4 NEW COMMITMENTS FOR MAJOR FEDERAL CREDIT PROGRAMS CLASSIFIED BY TYPE OF ASSISTANCE, MAJOR AGENCY OR PROGRAM (IN MILLIONS OF DOLLARS)

AGENCY OR PROGRAM	1961 ACTUAL		1962 ESTIMATE		1963 ESTIMATE	
	Direct loans	Guarantees and insurance	Direct loans	Guarantees and insurance	Direct loans	Guarantees and insurance
Housing and Home Finance Agency:						
Federal National Mortgage Association	291	—	575	—	1,000	—
Urban Renewal Administration	77	194	119	304	149	394
Community Facilities Administration	389	—	538	—	558	—
Federal Housing Administration	130	10,457	193	12,698	248	13,904
Public Housing Administration	288	311	417	446	448	453
Veterans Administration	213	1,702	237	2,440	275	2,490
Department of Agriculture:						
Rural Electrification Administration	417	—	367	—	480	—
Farmers Home Administration	364	28	405	81	461	81
Commodity Credit Corporation	220	1,594	353	2,621	297	2,125
Department of Commerce:						
Area Redevelopment Administration	—	—	99	—	118	—
Maritime Administration	1	31	—	78	—	95
Civil Aeronautics Board	—	2	—	12	—	10
Interstate Commerce Commission	—	75	15	76	—	75
Expansion of defense production	—	69		64		58
Small Business Administration	281	18	437	51	476	124
Department of Health, Education, and Welfare	107	—	92	—	92	—
Export-Import Bank	1,189	146	919	307	822	408
Department of State: Agency for International Development	1,208	27	2,014	45	2,653	100
Total by type of assistance	5,175	14,654	6,780	19,223	8,077	20,317
Grand total	19,829		26,003		28,394	

SOURCE: *The Budget of the United States Government, Fiscal Year Ending June 30, 1963, 1962, p. 306.*

these fields are housing, farming, operation of small businesses, and economic development overseas. Table 4 shows the magnitude of these credit programs, the Federal agencies that carry them out, and the major purposes for which the Federal government provides credit.

The Federal government reinforces its effort to achieve these purposes through other quasi-public agencies that operate with private and public funds. They are listed in Table 5.

Those who oppose these credit programs criticize them, first, because they are designed to achieve goals to which the critics object (e.g., many in this country believe that our government should not concern itself with the economic development of countries overseas). Second, it is argued that these programs usurp activities that should be left to private business, i.e., to the banks or savings institutions.

Third, they are criticized on the grounds that in this way government interferes with the free functioning of the economy. For example, it is argued that the housing industry has become substantially dependent upon governmental decisions as to whether the interest rates on loans for home building shall be raised or lowered. Others criticize the lending activities of the Small Business Administration, which were expanded rapidly in the late fifties and early sixties, on the ground that by extending cheap credit government maintains

TABLE 5 OUTSTANDING LOANS FOR MAJOR QUASI-PUBLIC CREDIT PROGRAMS CLASSIFIED BY AGENCY AND PROGRAM (IN MILLIONS OF DOLLARS)

AGENCY	JUNE 30, 1960	JUNE 30, 1961
Farm Credit Administration:		
Banks for cooperatives	551	595
Federal intermediate credit banks	1,698	1,831
Federal land banks	2,487	2,728
Federal Home Loan Bank Board,		
Federal home loan banks	1,770	1,869
Federal Reserve Board of Governors,		
Federal Reserve banks	289	72
Housing and Home Finance Agency,		
Federal National Mortgage Association		
(secondary market operations)	2,600	2,522
Total	9,395	9,617

SOURCE: *The Budget of the United States Government, Fiscal Year Ending June 30, 1963, 1962, p. 306.*

inefficient businesses that would (and should) fail and cease to exist if it were not for this "governmental crutch."

The growth of these programs indicates that those who favor governmental lending have prevailed. Essentially their reasoning is that the Federal government by extending credit stimulates the demand for the products of industry and thus stimulates the growth of this country's economy. Those who support these programs also ask: Who would aid the economic development of the underdeveloped countries of the world if the Federal government did not? And where would the large sums required for rebuilding this country's large cities come from if not from the Federal government?

Such issues are and should be resolved by democratic debate and legislative action. The public administrator's task is, first, to recognize the impact of these programs on our free enterprise economy. Second, he must be expected to see that the expansion or contraction of the credit programs for which he is responsible (e.g., home building) are neatly articulated with all other Federal activities. Only thus will the total efforts of the Federal government achieve their objective of keeping unemployment down or prices stable.

TAX AND DEBT POLICIES AND THE ECONOMY

The management of the supply of money and credit made available through the banks and the provision of credit assistance by the Federal government should be (but has not always been) interrelated with the government's fiscal policies. By fiscal policies are meant those pertaining to expenditures, taxation, debt management, and credit control.

When the government spends less, raises taxes, sells securities to individuals (e.g., savings bonds), or limits the borrowing of business firms, it reduces the amount of money in the hands of consumers. When the government spends more, when it pays off the public debt that is in the hands of the public, or when it encourages borrowing by citizens, it effectively increases the money they have to spend or to invest.

The agency of the Federal government primarily concerned with taxation and debt management is the Department of the Treasury. Within the Treasury, the Secretary and his principal political officers —the Under Secretary, the Under Secretary (Monetary Affairs) whose province is "managing" the public debt, the assistant secretaries, and the Commissioner of Internal Revenue—regularly make or recommend decisions regarding taxes and the public debt that vitally affect the economy.

EFFECT OF TAXES ON THE ECONOMY   No taxes are neutral in their effect on the earning and spending of income, and some taxes, such as individual income taxes (which provide more than half of all revenue of the Federal government, see Table 6), have a different effect on the taxpayer than excise taxes, for example. There is general agreement that the decisions of the Federal government as to the taxes on which it will base its annual budget affect the demands for goods and services. By raising taxes it can depress the total economy, or particular segments of it; by lowering taxes it may alternatively stimulate the economy.

Naturally, then, the level of taxation and the kind of taxes used have long been a much-debated political issue. Traditionally the Republican party has stood for a relatively broadly based personal income tax that requires most citizens to pay some tax and limits the rates applied to large personal incomes and to corporation profits. The Democratic party, in contrast, has stood for higher exemptions (that is, exemptions of the first $1,000 or $1,200 of income to benefit citizens with low incomes) and higher tax rates on large incomes (e.g., $30,000 a year or more) and on corporation profits.

TABLE 6   BUDGET RECEIPTS (FISCAL YEARS, IN BILLIONS OF DOLLARS)

SOURCE	1961 ACTUAL	1962 ESTIMATE	1963 ESTIMATE
Individual income taxes	41.3	45.0	49.3
Corporation income taxes	21.0	21.3	26.6
Excise taxes	9.1	9.6	10.0
Estate and gift taxes	1.9	2.1	2.3
Customs	1.0	1.2	1.3
Miscellaneous receipts	4.1	3.5	4.2
Total	78.3	82.8	93.7
Deduct interfund transactions	.7	.7	.7
Total budget receipts	77.7	82.1	93.0

SOURCE: *The Budget of the United States Government, Fiscal Year Ending June 30, 1963*, 1962, p. 20.

The economic and political significance of taxes, hence, focused public attention on the recommendation of President Kennedy to the Congress in 1962 that the President be given authority "to make temporary countercyclical adjustments in the first bracket rate of the personal income tax." If given this authority he would be able, without the delay involved in seeking legislation, to affect demand by taking less income from all taxpayers, thus leaving them more purchasing power. Simultaneously, the President proposed two tax measures designed to encourage business firms to increase their investments in plant and equipment. The first was an investment tax credit and the second was a liberalization of depreciation allowances. Both would make it advantageous for business firms to replace old equipment or to buy new,. and thus to encourage other firms to build equipment. Most of the authority the President requested, however, was not granted by the Congress.

EFFECT OF THE DEBT ON THE ECONOMY   The management of the public debt includes determining when bonds shall be sold, at what interest rates, for what length of time money shall be borrowed, and when bonds shall be retired. When the public debt is as large as at present, and when the amounts of bonds issued and retired each year are as great, decisions on these issues markedly affect the flow of money through the economy.

In 1962 the total debt aggregated 295 billion dollars; the interest paid to holders of this debt approximated 9 billion dollars; and the outstanding public debt was increased during the year by 7 billion dollars, an amount proportionately less than the growth in this country's gross national product.

From one point of view these figures can be interpreted to mean that the nation owed somewhat more, but its total wealth grew even more than the debt, and so it was in better financial shape. Others argue that any increase in debt represents a burden on future generations of taxpayers and indicates that the government is "living beyond its means."

FEDERAL EXPENDITURES: TYPES AND EFFECTS

Unless the demand of consumers, producers, and government is sufficient to buy the goods and services produced each year, we have unemployment, recession, and no economic growth. When the demand of consumers, producers, and government exceeds this country's production we may suffer from inflationary booms. Therefore, increasingly since 1932, the Federal government has striven to adjust its expenditures, whether financed from year to year by taxes or by increasing the debt, to ensure a demand adequate to minimize unemployment and limit price changes and, hence, stabilize the economy. Thus, it strives to prevent the sequence of booms and recessions.

The peacetime annual expenditures of the Federal government reached approximately 100 billion dollars for the first time in 1963. To understand the effect of this expenditure upon the demand for goods and services and thus upon the American economy, the student of public administration must recognize five distinct kinds of expenditures. Each poses different kinds of administrative problems and has different effects upon the economy.

NORMAL FEDERAL OPERATIONS Of the Federal government's total expenditure, approximately 45 billion dollars per annum goes for the costs of operating such departments as Agriculture, Commerce, Defense, Justice (the courts), Interior, Labor, and Treasury (including paying interest on the public debt) and the support of such old established agencies as the U.S. Tariff Commission and the Civil Service Commission. This expenditure grows as government grows larger, as prices rise, and particularly as greater demands are put on the government for defense. In the aggregate this expenditure consumes over 10 per cent of all the goods and services that make up this country's gross national product.

GRANTS-IN-AID Every state and local government depends in substantial part on financial grants-in-aid from the Federal government. More than 10 billion dollars is expended annually for these grants.

Two-thirds of such grants-in-aid are made for two purposes: the provision of financial assistance to needy aged, blind, and other persons and the construction of highways. The financial assistance or welfare grants (administered by the Department of Health, Education, and Welfare) enable state and local governments to put approximately 3 billion dollars into the hands of needy persons, who use it to buy food, clothing, shelter, medical care, and other essentials. The payments to the states for the construction of highways increase the demand for many construction items (e.g., asphalt, cement, and road machinery).

Administration of these grants-in-aid involves much more than simply paying out to the individual states funds that Congress appropriates. It involves the setting of standards to govern how and for what purposes the states shall use these funds. And it comprehends the provision of leadership to the states, stimulating them to construct better roads or to provide more generously for the needy, to hire better-qualified men and women, to increase the efficiency of their organizations, and to conform with standards set by Congress indicating the purposes for which the funds are granted.

STIMULATION OR SUPPORT OF ESSENTIAL INDUSTRIES

> . . . in the course of our history, the Federal government has engaged in a variety of subsidy, and subsidylike programs. Originally they were limited substantially to assistance to transportation interests, to encourage foreign trade and domestic expansion and development; more recently subsidies have expanded to the point where few segments of our economy are completely unaffected by them.[5]

This statement, in a report of the Joint Economic Committee of the Congress illustrates another means by which the Federal government materially influences demand. By paying subsidies government increases the purchasing power of a large body of American consumers (e.g., the farm families) and the investments and activity of important businesses (e.g., shipping and air transport) and markedly increases governmental expenditures.

The major recipient of Federal subsidies is the farmer. He receives approximately 1.2 billion dollars annually for farm products purchased by the government for sales to foreign countries, approximately 1.5 billion dollars to support the price he obtains for food products, and at least 1 billion dollars more for other purposes.[6]

In addition to subsidies paid directly or indirectly to farmers, the Federal government makes substantial subsidies to other segments of the economy. The principal subsidies are for (*a*) the construction and operation of air navigation aids (900 million dollars), (*b*) the construction and operation of commercial ships (660 million dollars), (*c*) the support of state unemployment compensation programs (300 million

[5] *Subsidy and Subsidylike Programs of the U.S. Government, a Staff Report for the Joint Economic Committee*, 86th Cong., December, 1960.
[6] *Ibid.*, p. 21.

dollars), (d) for urban renewal (482 million dollars), and (e) for the construction of public housing for low-income families (190 million dollars).

GOVERNMENT PURCHASES Government is this country's principal buyer. In 1961 government (Federal, state, and local) purchases exceeded 100 billion dollars, comprising 20 per cent of the gross national product. A decade earlier, total government purchases took 13 plus per cent of the gross national product.[7]

Government now "contracts out" for many activities that it once performed with its own staffs, in its own offices, arsenals, and yards. In addition to contracting for the building of ships, planes, and missiles, and for the manufacture of desks, shoes, and many other items, it contracts for operations and economic research, for the training of military officers, for engineering services, and for the operation of laboratories and cafeterias. Indeed, the services contracted for range from planning, engineering, and supervision of the whole missile problem to the physical distribution of all Air Force publications and forms to bases at home and abroad.

When government does as large a part of the country's total shopping as now is the case, the consequences can be substantial. Eleven of this country's 100 largest corporations sold, in 1959, more than three-fourths of their total output to the Federal government.[8] Dozens of other and smaller corporations throughout the country are dependent upon this one customer and make decisions in operating their businesses to conform with regulations and the will of contracting officers; they are essentially "kept corporations." The structure of whole industries (e.g., aircraft, electronics, missiles, and jet engines)[9] and the welfare of geographical areas (southern California, south-

[7] For consideration of government purchases in relation to the national economy see testimony of Louis J. Paradiso, Assistant Director, Office of Business Economics, Department of Commerce, before the Joint Economic Committee Dec. 7, 1960, and article entitled "Federal Purchases," *Survey of Current Business*, October, 1960, pp. 5–6.

[8] For example, 85 per cent of Raytheon's 1959 sales of 494 million dollars were to the Federal government. Similarly, such companies as the Martin Company, Boeing, Lockheed, Aerojet-General, and many others derived half or more of their total sales from the Federal government.

[9] Sales of the six largest companies in the airframe industry have climbed from 833 million dollars in 1950 to 5.8 billion dollars in 1959 with over 80 per cent of total sales being made directly to government (*Aviation Week*, Dec. 26, 1960, pp. 79–80, and "The Plane Makers under Stress," *Fortune*, June and July, 1960).

eastern Ohio) are dependent upon the continuing placement of government contracts.

The methods used in awarding government contracts, the kinds of contracts (e.g., fixed-price versus cost-plus), and the variety of security, personnel, and other regulations attached will go far toward determining the nature of competition, levels of prices, wages and profits, and incentives that prevail in large segments of American business.

WELFARE SERVICES Since colonial times government in this country has expended tax funds to protect the orphaned, the widowed, the handicapped, the aged, and the unemployed. During the Depression of the thirties this activity of government was greatly expanded, and the Social Security Act was enacted. Payments were initially undertaken to provide succor for the needy; but the Depression demonstrated that the payment of benefits could simultaneously increase consumer purchasing power and increase the demand for goods and services.

Two agencies are responsible for administering the principal Federal benefit programs: the Bureau of Old Age and Survivors Insurance and the Veterans Administration. The former (BOASI) employs more than 30,000 people to keep the social security records, on the basis of which it determines the amount of the monthly benefit due to each of thousands of applicants that come into the 500 field offices of this Bureau throughout the United States. The Veterans Administration, through offices distributed throughout the United States, pays more than 3.7 billion dollars in compensation as pensions and allowances each year to eligible veterans of our armed forces.

Through these programs and grants to the states for public assistance and for unemployment compensation the Federal government redistributes a substantial portion of the total national income. In 1962, the total of benefit payments approximated 30 billion dollars. This aggregate sum represents much-needed income for the least fortunate and a flexible means (particularly the benefits for the unemployed) by which additional purchasing power is placed in the hands of families without incomes when a recession has set in and is cut off automatically when better times come.

THE BUDGETARY PROCESS

The government's taxing, spending, and lending programs and its program for the control of money and credit are brought together in the Federal budget. This annual document is essentially the government's plan for ascertaining that all governmental services favorably influence the economy; i.e., that they speed the growth of the GNP or raise the level of employment without causing inflation.

The Federal budget has two sides: the receipts side and the expenditures side. We described earlier the role of the Treasury in determining what taxes shall be used. In framing each annual budget the staff of the Treasury must forecast the collections for each tax. The Congress need act on these taxes only if changes in tax laws must be made.

On the other side, it is the Bureau of the Budget that assembles for the President estimates of the amounts needed to support all activities of the Federal government. In this task the first step is the development of estimates as to the sums required by each department and agency. The second step is the review of these estimates by the

The budget dollar. (SOURCE: *The Budget of the United States Government, Fiscal Year Ending June 30, 1963*, page 32.)

WHERE IT COMES FROM . . .

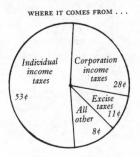

WHERE IT GOES . . .

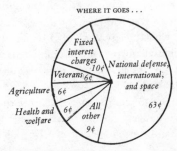

Fiscal year 1963 estimate

Congress and the enactment of appropriation laws. Together these two steps can be said to be the heart of the operations of the Federal government.

The budget is the principal tool the President uses to coordinate the activities of all executive departments and agencies to achieve the goals he sets each year. Equally important, it provides for a stocktaking by the head of each department and agency as to what has been accomplished, and what is planned for the year ahead. It provides for a thorough appraisal of the agency's operations and plans by the Bureau of the Budget, acting for and under the direction of the President. Finally, it provides for a thorough examination of the plans, work programs, and administrative performance of each agency by the legislature.

SETTING GOALS AND ACHIEVING COORDINATION   The task of coordinating the efforts of almost two hundred separate agencies is one of the President's year-round jobs. Annually the President in his State of the Union address, his budget message, and his economic report, and through other messages, states to the Congress and to the public his program for the fiscal year ahead. These are political documents. They constitute his assessment of what needs to be done in the light of prevailing international and domestic conditions, and for which he believes he can muster popular and political support.

In framing the program that these messages outline, the President consults with members of his Cabinet, the heads of agencies, legislative leaders, and other counselors. But the principal agencies upon which he depends to assess and interrelate the advice he receives are the Council of Economic Advisers and especially the Bureau of the Budget.

The Council is essentially the President's economic navigator. For example, in 1961 the Council advised the President (the Congress and the public) that there had been a gap between what the country could produce and what it actually did produce during the preceding five years. It attributed this gap in substantial part to government's failure to spend enough. Its advice was reflected in the budget the President released in January, 1962.

It is the Bureau of the Budget that does the major job of coordination, while the budget is being prepared, between August and January of each year, and during the balance of each year as its staff observes the operations of each agency. Its first step in the annual budget-making process is to issue guidelines to all agencies indicating the general limits of their budgets.

STOCKTAKING WITHIN EACH AGENCY   The task of preparing the budget for a department or agency is essentially the task of appraising what is being done in each unit and determining what should be done during the next year within the President's guidelines. Once the program is determined, the funds needed to pay the salaries of staff; to meet expenses for travel, rent, supplies, and other purposes; and to support grants to the state governments or contracts with private suppliers must be carefully estimated. The final budget is prepared in the form of "the justification books," which provide a detailed enumeration of what is requested and why.

In the typical department or agency this means that under the guidance of a budget officer, each bureau, office, and division prepares its own budget. These requests for funds along with written explanations or justifications for each item are reviewed by the budget officer and his staff. Hearings may be held by the head of the department or agency at which the bureau, office, or division heads are asked to justify their requests. After such review as the department head prescribes the budget is prepared by the budget officer and submitted to the Bureau of the Budget about September 15.

Unfortunately, the process of preparing and reviewing the budget seldom is used by busy department and agency heads to take stock of the operations and plans of each unit for which they are responsible. Too often the process is simply an effort to build persuasive explanations for the increases requested by each unit.

APPRAISAL BY THE BUREAU OF THE BUDGET   The Bureau of the Budget includes on its staff many of the ablest civil servants. They are organized into divisions that specialize in the work of agencies within specific fields (e.g., the Military Division concentrates, the year round, on the activities of the Department of Defense, the AEC, and NASA).

Their task is to appraise each segment of each departmental budget in terms of two criteria. Is it in accord with the President's program; i.e., does it emphasize those activities on which the President has indicated he proposes to place emphasis in the particular year? Does it reflect economical management of departmental affairs?

The appraisal of the Bureau of the Budget is accomplished through relatively formal hearings. Representatives of the department appear at the Bureau's offices at a designated time, usually in October or November. The department or agency head usually makes an opening statement describing the departmental request and stressing the particular requests for increased funds he regards as urgent. During subsequent hours or days (the hearings for a department may extend over a week or more) the Bureau's staff will "examine" (i.e., pose questions to) the representatives of each bureau in the department. These questions reflect their study of the budget since its receipt about September 15.

After these hearings the examining staffs formulate recommendations. The Director and his immediate staff must then weigh and balance these recommendations in preparing a total budget for consideration by the President. The final decisions as to the size and makeup of the budget are the President's, but the importance of recommendations of the Bureau of the Budget is large. The President alters the budget as recommended to him. But the magnitude of the budget dictates that he accept in principal part what his budget director recommends. Thus, it is in the Bureau of the Budget that decisions are formulated as to how large portions of this country's resources are allocated. In this process, and subject to revision by Congress, decisions are made concerning how much of this country's manpower and natural resources is used to build missiles or schools, how much goes for subsidy payments to farmers or for housing for city dwellers and for the various other programs of the Federal government.

UNDERSTANDING THE FEDERAL BUDGET In order to understand the budget of his government the citizen must recognize three facts not clear on the surface.

1. The expenditures authorized for any particular year do not tell the whole story. Each department or agency is not only authorized to spend designated amounts but is authorized to incur specified "new obligations." For example, when the building of the Saturn missile was first proposed, it was realized that it would cost more than 1 billion dollars and would require at least five years. In the first year NASA was authorized to spend about 100 million dollars. But it was also authorized to incur "new obligations" (let us say 200 million dol-

lars) that would be paid in future years. Such authorizations are a realistic recognition that the Federal government's business cannot be handled on a year-by-year basis.

2. Large parts of the Federal budget can be changed very little from year to year. Those who cry for economy in Federal expenditure seldom recognize that each successive President inherits the necessity of making large expenditures which he can little influence. The amount of "new obligations" authorized by his predecessor determine, in considerable part, what he must budget for. When Kennedy questioned whether the B-70 bomber should be built, he was confronted with the fact that hundreds of millions of dollars had been spent on its design and development, and contracts had been let for

TABLE 7 FEDERAL-AID BUDGET AND TRUST FUND
EXPENDITURES BY AGENCY (IN MILLIONS OF DOLLARS)

AGENCY	1961 ACTUAL	1962 ESTIMATE	1963 ESTIMATE
Executive Office of the President	12.5	1.2	—
Funds appropriated to the President	13.4	13.9	10.8
Department of Agriculture	685.4	897.3	1,038.5
Department of Commerce	2,623.1	3,055.6	3,321.6
Department of Defense—Military	—	19.6	134.7
Department of Defense—Civil	1.5	1.6	22.7
Department of Health, Education, and Welfare	2,891.0	3,389.4	3,746.7
Department of the Interior	114.9	120.8	130.1
Department of Labor	369.3	380.6	403.1
Department of State	1.4	9.0	8.0
Treasury Department	25.0	26.8	27.0
Federal Aviation Agency	64.8	81.2	76.0
General Services Administration	1.2	.7	1.3
Housing and Home Finance Agency	407.3	567.3	857.7
Veterans Administration	9.0	8.8	8.8
Other independent offices	15.7	19.9	27.5
District of Columbia*	47.9	87.2	82.1
Total	7,283.4	8,680.8	9,896.6

* Represents Federal payments, contributions, and loans to the District of Columbia for operations in capital improvements.
SOURCE: *The Budget of the United States Government, Fiscal Year Ending June 30, 1963,* 1962, p. 342.

work to be done in subsequent years. The size of the public debt and interest rates fixed by his predecessors determine what he must budget for interest on the debt. Legislation enacted decades ago dictates that at least another tenth of the total budget must be provided for grants-in-aid to the states (see Table 7).

The Federal government so far has avoided an additional difficulty that tends to make public budgets inflexible. A substantial part of state revenues are earmarked for particular activities; automobile and gasoline taxes, for example, are usually earmarked for highways. Activities supported by earmarked revenues largely escape budgetary review by the state legislature and the governor and do not compete with other government programs for appropriations out of the general fund. Earmarked revenues, however, make it impossible for the governor and the legislature to allocate available funds in accordance with their judgments as to the demonstrated needs of each governmental program. Fortunately little Federal revenue is earmarked for particular activities.

3. The annual Federal budget does not reflect all governmental expenditures. More than 27 billion dollars is expended annually from trust funds. This expenditure is not included in the annual administrative budget. These expenditures are reviewed by the Bureau of the Budget and are annually reported to the Congress and to the public as part of the total cash budget of the Federal government; i.e., the cash budget includes both the administrative budget and trust fund receipts and expenditures.

The largest single trust fund expenditure is from the Federal Old Age and Survivors Insurance Trust Fund for payments to beneficiaries, i.e., retired workers, their widows, or survivors. Other expenditures are to disabled workers, to the unemployed, and to veterans. The other major trust fund expenditure is to state governments for highway construction. Each of these trust funds, as Table 7 reveals, is supported by receipts from special sources, e.g., the social security payroll taxes.

By these trust funds the Federal government essentially underwrites its commitment to make payments to those who have contributed through social security payroll taxes and to complete highway programs for which planning and construction take a period of years. In addition, government can count on these payments to have some effect on balancing the ups and downs in our economy.

THE LEGISLATIVE ROLE

The Congress plays a large and important role in making the budget. Its principal, although not sole, agents in exercising this influence are the Joint Committee on the Economic Report, the appropriations committees, and the tax levying committees, i.e., the Ways and Means Committee of the House and the Finance Committee of the Senate.

The Joint Economic Committee of the Congress studies the economic situation and outlook, examines many current proposals for stimulating economic recovery or growth, and presents, in its annual report, recommendations on fiscal and monetary policies and on such matters as tax reform, the balance of payments, and the management of the public debt. The committee's advice has often been given little weight by the appropriations and tax levying committees. But the Joint Committee appears to be increasingly influential in focusing congressional and public attention on this country's uppermost economic problems.

THE MECHANICS OF EXPENDITURE CONTROL It is a principle of all democratic governments that no taxes may be levied or public funds expended without the authorization of the legislature.[10] Through its "power of the purse," the Congress exercises its principal control over the executive branch.[11] The appropriations committees exercise this control.

The authorization of expenditures by the legislature involves two distinct steps: (1) the program or activity must be authorized by law; and (2) funds must be appropriated to carry on authorized activities. State and local governments customarily authorize activities in broad legislation. Federal legislation authorizing government programs is often highly detailed. Authorizing legislation specifies not only objectives, but also the specific activities that may be carried on and the amount that may be spent. On some occasions such legislation limits the carrying on of such activities to a specified period of time.

[10] Article I, Section 9, of the Constitution provides that "No money shall be drawn from the Treasury, but in consequence of appropriations made by law. . . ." Most state constitutions have similar provisions.

[11] Alexander Hamilton observed in No. 30 of *The Federalist:* "Money is, with propriety, considered as the vital principle of the body politic; as that which sustains its life and motion, and enables it to perform its most essential functions."

THE INFLUENCE OF APPROPRIATIONS COMMITTEES The appropriations committees of Congress are regarded as the most powerful committees of Congress. They are the largest committees in each house. The House Appropriations Committee consists of 50 members and that of the Senate, 27; each utilizes 12 or more subcommittees, and each subcommittee has a staff to assist it.

Members of Congress ordinarily serve for several terms before being assigned to the appropriations committee. After being chosen they usually continue to serve on the committee as long as they remain in Congress. In 1959 the members on the House Committee had had an average of 8.14 years' service, and members of the Senate Committee, 7.44 years. Several members had served for more than 20 years, and two members, more than 30. Through long service and through visiting field installations of the departments between sessions, members acquire considerable knowledge of the work of the departments whose budgets they review.

The appropriations subcommittees of the two houses conduct lengthy hearings on the budgets of the departments assigned to them; the House conducts such hearings in "executive session," the Senate Committee, sometimes in public session. The House hearings may extend over several weeks or months. The head of each department or agency customarily makes a general statement at the start of the hearings outlining the plans and policies of the department and its financial needs. The chiefs of bureaus and other department officers follow and are questioned in detail about plans and estimates. The hearings of the larger departments often fill 2,000 printed pages of testimony, not including "off the record" passages.

Formerly the subcommittees devoted much attention to detailed items, such as the personnel of individual field offices, expenditures for travel and supplies, and other administrative costs. Today the hearings more often are devoted to a review of programs, future plans, and policies rather than to small items of expenditure. This trend has been encouraged by the adoption of the "performance" type of budget, which focuses attention on the broad goals to be achieved (e.g., the building of interstate highways) rather than on objects of expenditures such as the number of secretaries assigned to the office of a division chief in the Bureau of Public Roads.

In addition to the budget estimates, which show expenditures for the last fiscal year, estimated expenditures for the current year, and requested funds for the next fiscal year, each department submits the explanatory statements, or "justification books," which have been revised after review by the Bureau of the Budget. These provide the subcommittee members and their staff with detailed explanations of each program, its administration, future plans, and estimates of funds needed. They provide the basis for the questions propounded to department witnesses.

It is uncommon for any witness to appear in opposition to department budget requests. Citizen groups, chambers of commerce, and other organizations often testify in support of local public works projects or government activities of special interest to them. The appropriations committees receive few suggestions for specific reductions in the budget. Taxpayer groups that urge greater economy in government seldom propose specific reductions in government activities. The largest reductions are those made by the Bureau of the Budget and the President, rather than by legislative committees.

In passing on the budget the appropriations committees make the following distinct but closely related determinations: (1) they allocate available funds among the various departments, agencies, and programs; (2) they review the programs administered by the departments and make policy decisions; and (3) they inquire into departmental administration to ascertain whether government programs are being administered efficiently, economically, and in accordance with legislative policies. There are seldom sufficient funds to meet all demands, and the legislature must decide how funds will be allocated and where cuts or increases will be made in the executive budget. The recommendations of the appropriations committees are customarily adopted by the Congress with few changes.

In voting appropriations the legislature and especially its appropriations committees make many decisions which significantly supplement or alter laws drafted by other committees. Directives and instructions to the departments are often written into the appropriation acts or placed in the committee reports, which has about the same effect. In other instances, policy directions are given by the committees or their chairmen orally to department officers. Since the departmental officer must appear before the committees in successive years and seek essential appropriations, these oral directions carry considerable weight.

WEAKNESSES IN THE LEGISLATIVE APPROPRIATION PROCESS A major criticism of congressional action on the budget is that it does not consider the Federal budget as a whole. The appropriations are voted in a series of 15 or more appropriation acts each year, each taken up at different times by separate and largely independent subcommittees and considered largely apart from the overall financial position of the government. Revenue measures are passed on by other committees in each house and are taken up at other times. Moreover, practically all standing committees (other than the appropriations committees) significantly affect the annual financial program by reporting legislation that authorizes new or enlarged government expenditures.

Legislative responsibility, in short, is widely diffused. The relative financial requirements of the various departments are not balanced against one another. The total need is not viewed in relation to revenues available or in relation to economic conditions.

The Congressional Reorganization Act of 1946 provided for a so-called "legislative budget" to correct this glaring weakness in legislative action. Congress was supposed to fix a ceiling on expenditures early in each session to guide the actions of the appropriations and revenue committees. This plan never worked successfully and was soon abandoned.

A related reform frequently urged is the adoption of a single consolidated appropriation act in place of the 15 or more acts which Congress passes each year. This reform would enable Congress to pass upon the entire expenditure budget at one time. The plan was tried in 1950 but was abandoned the following year as impracticable.

The organization and procedures by which Congress passes upon finance worked reasonably well when the Budget and Accounting Act of 1921 was adopted and when the annual budget was around three billion dollars, and had little impact on the economy. They are poorly adapted to today's budget, which is more than thirty times as large, vastly more complex, and affects both the domestic and world economy. While executive budgetary procedures have undergone many refinements since 1921 and the Bureau of the Budget has developed into a central financial management agency, congressional procedures remain relatively unchanged.

It is high time Congress improved its budgetary review processes. This does not mean that Congress should strive to supplant the executive in its formulation of the budget. That would be a step backward. Congress and the President each have essential roles in the determination of financial policies. But unless Congress does reform its budgetary review processes, greater control over Federal finance will accrue inevitably to the executive branch.

PUBLIC VERSUS PRIVATE ENTERPRISE

Contrary to what many businessmen assume, the Constitution did not fix any inflexible dividing line as to what should be done by government and what should be left to private enterprise. And the growth of population, the advance of technology that makes possible a better standard of living for all, the concentration of people in cities, and the persistent necessity of providing for the national defense—these forces and others—ensure that government will continue to grow and expand. As it grows in size and in the variety of activities performed it will inevitably exercise greater influence over the functioning of the economy.

The extent of the influence it exercises in striving to maintain economic stability and to promote economic growth was strikingly brought to the attention of the American people in April, 1962, when President Kennedy in a press conference vigorously criticized the steel companies for having raised prices. In subsequent days he had the Federal departments and agencies take a number of indirect actions to cause the steel companies to rescind their action. Within five days they did.

In summary, the President had declared that the price of steel affects the price of the house, car, appliances, and many other consumer items every family must have, and that an increase in its price at that time would be inflationary. The steel companies countered that an increased price and increased profits were required to enable them to build modern furnaces and equipment so that they might increase their productivity and compete effectively with foreign steel producers.

Both the President and the steel companies were right in their contentions. Those contentions highlight two sides of an important issue: Should government exercise any control over the prices of basic commodities? And if it need influence such prices, can it do this without unduly restricting the freedom of businessmen to manage their own affairs? This issue grows out of the rapid development of the country as a highly industrialized society. And it reflects the growing responsibilities of public administrators in this society.

Review Questions

1. In weighing the counterarguments that the Federal government can and cannot influence the growth of the United States economy, what elements of the economy and what measures would you look to?

2. What tools does the Federal Reserve System use to exercise control over the supply of money and credit?

3. What are the principal purposes for which the Federal government extends credit and why does it extend credit for these purposes? What arguments are brought against such activity on the part of government?

4. Can you suggest what effect on the economy would result from the raising or from the lowering of each of the five principal tax sources listed in Table 6?

5. Of the five distinguishable types of expenditures made by the Federal government what is the likely effect on the economy of raising or lowering each? Through which types of expenditures does the Federal government strive to overcome recessions?

6. What is meant by the term "budget"? What is the function of the Federal budget? What is the function of the staff of the Bureau of the Budget?

7. How much freedom does the President have from year to year in modifying the budget of the Federal government? To what extent does the budget reflect the total costs of the Federal government?

8. In the light of the large sums being appropriated and the substantial taxes being levied are the processes used by the Congress in arriving at its decisions on the budget adequate?

9. In your opinion do the changes wrought by population growth, advance in technology, the persistence of the cold war, and the concentration of people living in major cities warrant the extent to which government now influences or controls many segments of the economy?

10. In your opinion was the President justified in using the power of his office to force the steel companies to forego raising their prices in 1962?

REGULATING PRIVATE ENTERPRISE

Chapter 7

THE ROOTS OF REGULATION

Competition, we Americans have long reasoned, ensures that, while each individual and each business pursues his (or its) self-interest, the interests of all are protected. But experience has taught that there can be too much competition. Excessive or unfair competition may injure producers, workers, or competitors.

Hence, government has long intervened to substitute its own controls where competition has not controlled effectively. It has intervened in those industries (e.g., the public utilities) where the duplication of facilities is economically wasteful. It has intervened to ensure the safety of customers (e.g., by regulating food and drugs) or to protect workers (e.g., by establishing minimum wages and safe working conditions). And it has intervened, in other instances, to preserve and promote fair competition (e.g., by passing the antitrust laws).[1]

Such intervention in the free functioning of the economy is called regulation, and it is one of the most important and pervasive activities of the Federal government. The range of regulatory activities has steadily increased in recent decades, until in 1960 they affected almost all business enterprises, in some degree, and almost every significant aspect of the American society. Regulatory activities pose unique organizational and administrative problems. To understand these problems, one must learn how and why these activities came into being, the nature of the Federal agencies that exist to regulate, what they do, how they carry out their functions, and the principal criticisms made of their operations.

THE EVOLUTION OF REGULATION

Early examples of government regulation were laws requiring shopkeepers to use standard weights and measures, and proprietors of restaurants and taverns to maintain standards of cleanliness. Such laws were enacted because competition failed to protect society against short weights or unsanitary food.

As the American economy became more complex other needs for governmental intervention emerged. These additional needs, in many instances, could not be met by the simple passing of a law. They required the day-to-day application of a law in a technical field (e.g., aircraft transportation) and the adjustment of its impact on customers or on the industry. Hence, after deciding to regulate an industry (e.g., radio broadcasting or security trading), the legislature simultaneously established an agency to administer the law and gave the agency authority to interpret the law and to decide how the law or the rules should be applied, that is, to adjudicate cases.

[1] For further consideration of the comprehensive impact of government regulation and the causes giving rise to the continued expansion of the role of regulatory agencies, see the "Landis Report," a *Report on Regulatory Agencies to the President-elect*, printed for the use of the Committee on the Judiciary, U.S. Government Printing Office, Washington, 1960.

REGULATION OF TRANSPORTATION

These steps, intervention by law and then the establishment of an administrative agency to apply the law, were first taken in the field of transportation. In the early 1800s the state governments encouraged the building of railroads by grants of land, loans of money, and liberal charters. Later the Federal government promoted their development in similar ways. Regulation, in the narrower sense of control, came later. It came in response to two forces: the threat of economic collapse by some railroads that had overbuilt and cutthroat competition among the railroads. The latter gave rise to exorbitant charges in some instances, to discrimination against some shippers and some localities, and still other forms of unfair competition.

The state governments attempted to regulate the railroads but were unsuccessful. Their lack of success was due to the strength of financial interests backing the railroads and the fact that the railroads extended beyond individual state borders. Early state railroad commissions were granted only limited powers and usually had wholly inadequate staffs. The Supreme Court held in the *Wabash* case (*Wabash, St. Louis & Pacific Railroad v. Illinois*, 1886) that the states could not regulate commerce between states, thus enabling the railroads to escape from state controls.

This decision led Congress to create the Interstate Commerce Commission in 1887. At first its powers were limited. It could receive complaints and issue orders declaring practices of the railroads to be discriminatory or rates to be unreasonable, but it had no authority to fix rates or to enforce its orders.

Subsequently, the ICC was authorized to act on its own initiative rather than on the basis of complaints filed, to fix rates, to issue orders stipulating operating practices, to pass upon proposed mergers of railroads, and to recommend loans and other financial aid for "sick" railroads. In addition, and importantly, since the early 1930s it has been responsible for relating rail and other forms of transportation— bus, truck, water, and air—and for regulating interstate bus and truck carriers, and water carriers operating on domestic canals and rivers.

Since the earliest days of this nation, government has encouraged oceangoing shipping by providing mail subsidies, by imposing heavy duties on competing foreign shipping, by building, operating, and selling ships, by loaning funds for ship construction, by requiring that government-financed cargo be shipped in American vessels, and by vast expenditures for improving the navigability of rivers, canals, and harbors.

In recent years these and related functions have been discharged by three agencies. The U.S. Maritime Commission came into being in 1936. It inherited authority to grant subsidies for ship construction and operation,[2] and it was given power to regulate ocean carriers, that is, to consider complaints of shippers or of passengers as to discrimination in the forwarding of freight or furnishing docks or other facilities in ports. In 1950 the Commission was succeeded by the Federal Maritime Board within the Department of Commerce. And in 1962 Reorganization Plan No. 7 converted the Board into the Federal Maritime Commission and made the agency independent of the Department of Commerce. Authority to grant subsidies for ship construction and operation was retained in the Department of Commerce.

The relation of the Federal government to air transportation began with the Air Mail Act of 1925. This act provided for contracting with private companies to carry mail by aircraft. The air-transport industry has been heavily dependent upon postal payments since then, and the payments have in most years exceeded the government's receipts from airmail.

The growth of air transportation and continuing heavy losses by the air carriers resulted in enactment of the Civil Aeronautics Act of 1938. This act established the Civil Aeronautics Administration within the Department of Commerce and entrusted it with promotional and operating as well as regulatory responsibilities. It authorized the CAA to develop this country's airways, to plan and stimulate the building of airports, to enforce safety licensing and traffic, to investigate accidents, to assign routes to airlines, and to fix the rates they might charge. Two years later, Congress established the semi-independent Civil Aeronautics Board to replace the Air Safety Board, which had been primarily concerned with the investigation of air crashes. The CAB was given authority to set airmail payments and subsidies, to allot routes, to fix rates, to ensure safety, and to pass on the merger or combination of airlines.

In 1958 the Federal Aviation Agency was established outside the Department of Commerce to regulate and control the use of air

[2] This Commission succeeded the U.S. Shipping Board established in 1916, under the pressure of World War I, to purchase, construct, and operate ships.

space by military and civilian airplanes, to provide navigation facilities, to perform safety functions formerly entrusted to CAB, and to take over all activities of CAA. At that time, CAB became wholly independent of the Department of Commerce.

Through these three agencies—the ICC, the FMC, and the CAB—and their predecessors, the Federal government has spent billions of dollars in promoting the development of transportation. It has simultaneously developed methods for regulating routes, rates, operating practices, and safety provisions. But, as President Kennedy told the Congress in April, 1962, the machinery for governmental regulation is "a chaotic patchwork of inconsistent and often obsolete legislation and regulation" that makes for "excessive, cumbersome and time-consuming regulatory supervision" that "shackles and distorts managerial initiative." He argued for placing "greater reliance on the forces of competition and less reliance on the restraints of regulation." And he pointed to five underlying factors:

1. The excess capacity of the railroads (70,000 miles of railway that are not needed).

2. Increasing urbanization and the inability of transport to carry commuters.

3. Chaotic and obsolete legislation forcing freight and passenger rates to remain above earlier levels and preventing the airlines from offering competitive rates or merging to build stronger and more effective competitors, e.g., rail with air.

4. The inequality that ensues from the fact that railroads must spend more for their rights-of-way than other major forms of transportation. Other forms of transport—aircraft, automobiles, and barges—are provided by government with publicly maintained or subsidized highways, airports, and waterways.

5. Railroad transport must have more effective research so that it may improve its service. The unions, a managerial lethargy that discourages advanced technology, and a general lack of profits and funds have discouraged all programs for capital expenditures.

REGULATION OF UTILITIES

The power and communications industries are also "affected with the public interest"; i.e., the public is heavily dependent upon the service they provide. Each is, in some degree, a "natural monopoly": a television channel can be used by only one broadcaster in each area; in other industries (e.g., telephone), competition being wasteful, a single company is granted a franchise to provide exclusively the service required in a city or town.

Like the railroads, the early electric companies were recognized, in the 1880s, as providing a prospectively valuable service. Hence, the early electric companies were given liberal franchises authorizing them to serve exclusively certain towns or cities. These franchises constituted the first effort of the local or state governments to regulate such companies.

Regulation by franchise did not work. Within 20 years substantial criticism had grown up; customers complained of high rates and exorbitant profits. To meet these complaints the first state utility commissions were established in New York and Wisconsin. Since then each state has established a commission to regulate electric utilities.

The Federal government entered the field of regulation through its responsibility for the conservation of water power and for facilitating the free flow of traffic over inland waterways. The Federal Water Power Act, enacted in 1920, established the Federal Power Commission and authorized it to license power developments on public lands, reservations, and any navigable stream.

Subsequently, the FPC's authority was extended to regulate the interstate transmission of electric energy, to fix rates, and to coordinate the planning and interrelation of electric facilities throughout the nation. Still later, the FPC was assigned the tasks of regulating the transportation and sale of natural gas.

In substantial part, the Commission's establishment, and its extension of authority, was in response to the weakness of the state commissions. Their weakness was due, in large part, to the growth of the interstate transmission of electric power, and to the emergence of holding company ownership. Each of these factors tended to enable electric utility companies to escape regulation by any state, or to accept regulation only by those states that dealt with them most liberally.

The communications industries—telegraph, telephone, radio, television—went through similar experiences. By nature these industries involved operations extending over many states. Hence, the Western Union Telegraph Company and the American Telephone and Telegraph Company (the Bell System) each grew, through the consolidation of many small companies, to cover the entire nation. Their growth was made possible and furthered by their holding of valuable patents.

The states, through their regulatory commissions, strove to control these large and growing companies in the provision of services which, between 1875 and 1920, became increasingly valuable to the American people. Regulation of the communication industries was ineffective, as was regulation of electric utilities, because of the interstate nature of the service and the national ownership of these companies.

As a consequence, in 1934, the Federal Communications Commission was established and made responsible for regulating the already declining telegraph industry, for the fixing of "long line" telephone rates, and for regulating the relations of the national AT&T with its local operating companies in individual states.

But new problems have a way of arising, and the influence exercised by radio and television, which reach 90 per cent of all homes, is so large that in the sixties there has been an urgent public demand to influence both the national networks and the stations to improve the programs they broadcast. Yet the FCC has found no effective way to accomplish this; it can revoke the license of a station, but this action, depriving the station owner of valuable property and of a livelihood, is so drastic that it has not been done. The FCC cannot substitute its judgment for the station manager's as to what programs he should broadcast. Hence, the problem remains.

REGULATION OF BUSINESS STRUCTURE AND PRACTICES

TO PRESERVE AND PROMOTE COMPETITION   Four important statutes have been enacted by the Federal government to preserve and promote competition among business enterprises.

The Antitrust Division of the Department of Justice is responsible for enforcing the antitrust provisions of these laws: the Sherman Antitrust Act of 1890, the Clayton Act of 1914, the Federal Trade Commission Act of 1914, and the Robinson-Patman Act of 1936. Its staff of 500, of which most are lawyers, investigates possible violations, conducts grand jury proceedings, prepares and prosecutes antitrust cases, and negotiates and enforces final decrees. This staff handles both criminal prosecutions to punish violators for restraints of and monopolization of trade, and civil proceedings and negotiations through which it strives to reestablish competitive conditions.[3] It

[3] During the fiscal year 1959 some 66 antitrust cases were closed, 124 new investigations opened, 126 old ones closed, and over 950 mergers or corporate acquisitions reviewed.

negotiates agreements with the defendant business firms, called "consent decrees," in which the defendant agrees to discontinue certain practices objected to by the government. Such consent decrees have played an important role, over the years, in maintaining a competitive environment.

The other major agency concerned with business structure and practice, the Federal Trade Commission, is an independent commission of five members appointed by the President. Half of its staff of 800 works in 10 field offices developing evidence of violations or negotiating with businesses to secure voluntary compliance. The headquarters staff investigates and prosecutes cases of price-fixing, price discrimination, economic coercion, exclusive dealing, false advertising, and other unfair practices and administers regulations requiring the "truthful labeling" of textiles, furs, and dangerously flammable wearing apparel marketed in interstate commerce. Finally, this staff negotiates with law offenders, holds "Trade Practice Conferences" with representatives of industries, and issues statements of advice and interpretation of its policies for businessmen and lawyers.

In general, the Antitrust Division of the Department of Justice and the FTC have tried to minimize the duplication of effort by notifying each other when proceedings are started. In addition, some agreement has been reached that in administering the merger provisions of the Clayton Act certain industries will be covered by the Antitrust Division and others by the FTC. But both businessmen and the staffs of these two agencies have suffered because the exact division of responsibilities between them has never been made clear.

TO PREVENT CUTTHROAT COMPETITION   In striving to prevent false advertising and unfair or dangerous marketing and labeling practices, the FTC not only protects the consumer against shoddy or dangerous merchandise, but protects the reputable manufacturers from having to compete with falsely labeled products. Similarly, the Food and Drug Administration of the Department of Health, Education, and Welfare, through the various food, drug, and cosmetic acts,[4] and the Packers and Stockyards Administration of the Department of Agriculture, through other legislation, are responsible for ensuring that the customer can buy products that meet reasonable standards of

[4] The Federal Food, Drug, and Cosmetic Act, the Tea Importation Act, the Import Milk Act, the Federal Caustic Poison Act, and the Fluid Milk Act.

purity and are truthfully and informatively labeled and also protect ethical businesses from unfair competition.

For example, the FDA headquarters staff in Washington supervises 40 inspection stations staffed with chemists, inspectors, and assistants. The staffs inspect food, drug, packing, and other business houses; collect samples of their products for laboratory analysis; supervise the reconditioning or destruction of impure goods; initiate legal actions to prevent violations or to punish violators; and generally try to educate the public to comply with these laws. Unfortunately the field staffs are wholly inadequate in numbers to regulate the practices of three million business establishments subject to the food and drug laws.

REGULATION OF INVESTMENT

The Securities and Exchange Commission owes its origin to the development of the corporate form of organization and to the popularity of corporate securities as a form of investment. A century ago wealth was in the form of land, buildings, factories, or ships; by the 1930s the wealth of many Americans was in the form of stocks and bonds.

The collapse of the stock market in 1929 revealed abuses that had grown up as more and more Americans had come to invest or speculate in securities. A series of Senate hearings conducted from 1932 to 1934 uncovered numerous cases of incompetence, irresponsibility, and abuse of trust by the investment bankers that marketed securities to the public.

Two acts resulted: the Security Act of 1933 and the Securities Exchange Act of 1934. The first provided for the regulation of the issuers of securities and of the bankers that sell securities to the public. Essentially, it required that all companies and all distributors offering securities for public sale in interstate commerce disclose all financial data necessary to permit the buyer to evaluate the worth of the securities.

The second act extended regulation to control of the activities of the securities markets (e.g., the New York Stock Exchange) and established the Securities and Exchange Commission. The SEC, a bipartisan body of five members, was created to administer the two acts. In subsequent years, its authority was extended to regulate public utility holding companies, the over-the-counter security markets, investment trusts, and investment advisers. The nature of its organization is shown by the figure on the next page.

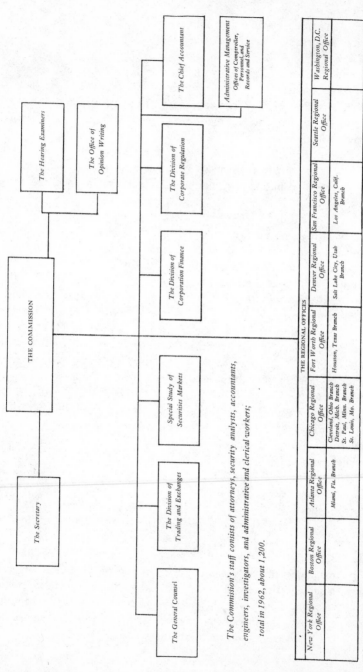

The Commission's staff consists of attorneys, security analysts, accountants, engineers, investigators, and administrative and clerical workers; total in 1962, about 1,200.

| THE COMMISSION |

| The Secretary |
| The General Counsel |
| The Hearing Examiners |
| The Office of Opinion Writing |
| The Chief Accountant |
| Administrative Management Offices of Comptroller, Personnel, and Records and Service |

| The Division of Trading and Exchanges |
| Special Study of Securities Markets |
| The Division of Corporation Finance |
| The Division of Corporate Regulation |

THE REGIONAL OFFICES

New York Regional Office	Boston Regional Office	Atlanta Regional Office	Chicago Regional Office	Fort Worth Regional Office	Denver Regional Office	San Francisco Regional Office	Seattle Regional Office	Washington, D.C. Regional Office
		Miami, Fla. Branch	Cleveland, Ohio Branch Detroit, Mich. Branch St. Paul, Minn. Branch St. Louis, Mo. Branch	Houston, Texas Branch	Salt Lake City, Utah Branch	Los Angeles, Calif. Branch		

The Securities and Exchange Commission.

The SEC has earned more general acceptance from the interests it regulates and more widespread approval from the public it protects than any other regulatory commission. It has become, in effect, the guardian of all who save and invest in publicly traded corporate securities. This role carries responsibilities that are growing both in volume and in kind; it is estimated that in the early sixties the number of shareholders increased each year by about 1⅓ million; simultaneously, during these years the SEC was confronted with such new problems as how to provide essential protection for the investor if and when the insurance companies are authorized to sell variable annuity contracts.

REGULATION AND LABOR RELATIONS

The regulation of labor relations had its origin in two analogous developments. First, industrialization has transformed the United States from a rural society in which most men lived and worked for themselves on farms to a society in which most men live in cities and work for others, in offices, plants, and factories. Second, the growth of unionism among working people has proceeded along with industrialization.

The right of workers to organize in unions and thus to strengthen their capacity to bargain with employers as to wages and conditions of work was for decades thwarted by "yellow dog contracts" under which employers hired workers on condition they would not join a union. Under the Sherman and Clayton antitrust acts workers who banded together to enforce their demands for higher wages or better conditions were sometimes determined to be engaged in an illegal conspiracy.

The Norris-LaGuardia Act of 1932 outlawed "yellow dog contracts," and the National Industrial Recovery Act of 1933 guaranteed working people the right to organize and to bargain collectively. This latter act was heralded by organized labor as a "magna charta"; hence, when other provisions of this act were declared unconstitutional by the Supreme Court, there was an urgent demand for its replacement. That demand gave birth to the National Labor Relations Act of 1935, the Wagner Act. That law set up machinery to enforce the employees' right to organize and to bargain collectively.

The machinery was headed by the three-man National Labor Relations Board whose task was (1) to investigate and decide alleged unfair practices by employers and (2) to decide cases involving questions as to who should represent workers as their bargaining agent.

The activities of the Board were the subject of controversy from its origin. During its early years (1935–1947) it was accused of a strong labor bias. This sentiment resulted in enactment, in 1947, of the Labor-Management Relations Act (popularly known as the Taft-Hartley Act) over the veto of President Truman. That act increased the size of the Board to five members but, more significantly, strengthened the rights of employers before the Board and included new and much controverted provisions designed to regulate the practices and internal operations of unions.

Other Federal agencies administer laws designed to protect the lowest-paid workers. Essentially, these laws say: Competition between employers and workers shall not be permitted to force their wages to a level that precludes decent living. The laws are the Fair Labor Standards Act of 1938 and the Walsh-Healey Public Contracts Act of 1936.

They are administered by the Wage and Hour Division and the Public Contracts Division, two divisions of the Department of Labor, consolidated in 1942 under a single administrator appointed by the President with the consent of the Senate. This agency's principal job is to see to it that employers subject to these Federal laws do not pay workers less than the hourly minimum of $1.25.

ADMINISTRATIVE MACHINERY FOR REGULATION

The foregoing synoptic retrospection of five broad sectors of the American economy indicates why and how administrative machinery for regulation has been developed within the Federal government. By the 1960s, a total of nine regulatory commissions existed:

CARRIER REGULATION

1887   Interstate Commerce Commission (ICC): rail, motor carriers, water carriers, and pipelines

1962   Federal Maritime Commission (FMC): water carriers

1938   Civil Aeronautics Board (CAB): air carriers

UTILITY REGULATION

1920   Federal Power Commission (FPC): electricity and natural gas

1933   Federal Communications Commission (FCC): telephone, telegraph, radio and television

BUSINESS STRUCTURE AND PRACTICES

1914   Federal Trade Commission (FTC): unfair trade practices

FINANCE AND CREDIT REGULATION

1934   Securities and Exchange Commission (SEC): investment bankers, trusts, and advisers, security exchanges, issues, holding companies

1913   Federal Reserve Board (FRB): money, credit, and member commercial banks (activities described in Chapter 6)

LABOR RELATIONS

1936   National Labor Relations Board (NLRB): unfair labor practices, collective bargaining

These agencies, together with units within several departments and agencies, particularly the departments of Agriculture; Commerce; Labor; Health, Education, and Welfare; and the Federal Aviation Agency, perform a distinctive governmental function.

But why has the Congress entrusted this function to the kind of agencies that now are known as regulatory commissions? First, the Congress followed the earlier experience of state governments with regulatory commissions. The states had attempted to regulate the activities of banks, insurance companies, and later, railroads through legislation. But experience proved that the state legislatures and their investigative committees had neither the time nor the skills to examine the affairs, inspect the books, or analyze periodic reports the legislation required. Hence, full-time and continuing commissions were established.

Second, the Congress recognized the need for expert and specialized staffs. It recognized that engineers, accountants, lawyers, and economists would be required, for example, to oversee the safety of operations and to evaluate the fairness of rates charged by railroads. It recognized that such staffs could best be assembled and directed by a continuing administrative agency.

Third, it was believed that administrative agencies possessing expert staffs could relieve private individuals of proving in court that they had been discriminated against or had been charged unreasonably for an essential service. The staffs could make investigations and assemble and present evidence that individuals could not possibly develop.

Fourth, these expert staffs could devise more efficient procedures for carrying on much of the work of regulation (e.g., issuing franchises to radio stations) and for assembling essential evidence (e.g., as to trading practices on a stock exchange) than the traditional and unspecialized legal processes of the courts. It was expected, hence, that the commissions' staffs would dispose of matters presented for adjudication more expeditiously and less expensively than could the courts. Moreover, and importantly, courts could only redress grievances; the commissions were given authority to set rates and to stipulate future practices.

Fifth, it was believed that multiheaded commissions, usually made up of representatives of two or more political parties, aided by an impartial civil service staff of experts would be free from undue influence by the parties to be regulated, e.g., the railroads, the television networks. Seven of the nine regulatory commissions are headed by bipartisan boards ranging in size from three to eleven members. The CAB, FPC, FTC, NLRB, and SEC each have five members; the FRB and the FCC have seven members each. Only the members of the FRB and the NLRB are selected without the necessity of maintaining a balance among members from the national parties.

WHAT REGULATORY AGENCIES DO

No two regulatory agencies perform all of the same functions. Nor do those that perform similar functions use identical forms of organization or methods. But four aspects of the work described by the general term "regulatory" that make the administration of these agencies distinctive can be identified and illustrated.

Most of the commissions (and such agencies as the Food and Drug Administration and the Wage and Hour Division) *enforce laws*. This enforcement includes preliminary investigation, prosecution, informal settlement, and administrative adjudication. The National Labor Relations Board, of all the commissions, is peculiarly a law enforcement agency. The standards of unfair practices are spelled out in the Labor-Management Relations (Taft-Hartley) Act. Thus, the NLRB is continually investigating complaints that employers or unions have violated provisions of this law, prosecuting in the courts those who their investigations disclose have or may have violated the law, or, alternatively, working out informal settlements that are agreed to by the employer and/or the union.

Most commissions also *make rules* and formulate policies. The Civil Aeronautics Board, for example, has established what is known as the "use it or lose it rule." This means that if an airline is granted the right to fly its planes over the route from Ithaca to Albany, New York, it must make the established number of runs between these two cities or give up the right to fly its planes over this route. The Federal Trade Commission similarly has issued rules as to what kinds of advertising are consistent with the textile- and fur-labeling acts, to guide those who sell such products.

The basic statutes creating the commissions specify in several instances that they shall *formulate broad plans* to govern the industries they regulate. For example, the CAB is required by statute to plan the development of a national system of civil air transport. Similarly, some contend that the ICC has a statutory obligation under Transportation Act of 1958 to plan for the survival of the commuter railroad in the face of automobile competition. The development by the FPC of a policy setting forth "area prices" below which sales of natural gas will be approved by an expedited procedure is another illustration of broad planning.

Some commissions (e.g., the FCC, FPC, ICC, and CAB) *regulate rates and grant licenses, certificates, and permits.* The FCC, for example, regulates the rates charged by the American Telephone & Telegraph Company for "long lines" service. It also grants licenses to the operators of small boats for the use of radio frequencies. Similarly, the Federal Power Commission regulates the rates charged for the sale of natural gas by producers and for the transmission of natural gas by pipeline companies. The Federal Trade Commission is authorized by statute to conduct investigations of the competitive practices of business firms and of entire industries; for example, it investigated chain store operations, the activities of public utility holding companies, and the marketing of antibiotics.

Several commissions are responsible for *promotional* efforts; most commissions perform certain *executive* activities. The Civil Aeronautics Board "promotes" the development of a nationwide civil air transport system. It does this in principal part by the granting of subsidies to airlines. Its promotional efforts are supplemented by those of the Federal Aviation Agency, which manages air traffic throughout the nation, plans and administers the program for the construction and financing of airports, and enforces standards as to the licensing of pilots and the maintenance of aircraft. Both the Civil Aeronautics Board and the Federal Aviation Agency perform the essential executive function of investigating accidents.

DISTINCTIVENESS OF
REGULATORY ADMINISTRATION

This summary of five distinct types of activities makes clear the breadth of the function performed by independent regulatory commissions. The distinctive character of these functions, however, is derived from two other facts. First, the commissions operate under broad, sometimes several, and even contradicting statutes. They are required to give specific meaning to the statutes they administer by issuing policies, making rules, or deciding cases.

Second, the commissions, except the Federal Reserve Board, make many decisions that vitally affect individual interest (e.g., the trader on the security exchange or the employer of organized workers). Most of their decisions may be appealed to the Federal courts. Hence their decisions must generally be based upon evidence placed in the record at a public hearing.

Because each commission performs the quasi-legislative task of translating generally stated statutes into policies and rules, and the quasi-judicial task of deciding cases by applying such statutes, policies, and rules to the interests of businesses and individuals, each is organized in a fashion quite distinct from the departments and agencies that perform a more conventional administrative job.

This organization is built around relatively large staffs of lawyers and hearing examiners, who preside at the many hearings and determine what shall go into the record of each case. They may make or recommend a decision. The hearing examiners act for the board that heads the agency; they relieve the boards of having to decide hundreds of cases which they simply do not have time to consider individually. Although the decisions of the hearing examiners are subject to appeal to the commissions, in the majority of cases they are accepted without appeal and become final. Hence the examiners, like the commissions which they serve, act in a quasi-judicial capacity, and are accorded substantial independence of supervision and direction by the Administrative Procedures Act. They are guaranteed security of tenure, even as are judges of Federal courts. All-in-all, the hearing examiner is a distinctive civil servant.

Each commission is headed by a board, because of the belief that the objectivity and impartiality of the decisions they must reach, as quasi-legislative and quasi-judicial agencies, will be better assured by three or more men of differing political faiths than by one man. Simultaneously, however, the existence of such boards makes it difficult for any one member, usually the chairman, to "run" the agency. Boards that serve well as tribunals are not efficient instruments for selecting division chiefs, choosing office space, making budgets, and performing similar administrative tasks. Yet all this is part of the task of running a regulatory commission.

The commissions are independent; i.e., they are not included within any one of the executive departments but are accountable (to the extent that they report at all) to the President. Other agencies, as for example, the Veterans Administration or the Atomic Energy Commission may be independent because of their size, the influence of a supporting pressure group, or the fact that their activities are largely unrelated to those of existing executive departments. But each is subject to direction and supervision by the President. The regulatory commissions have been made independent in order to endow these "administrative courts" with a freedom to "make law" under the statutes and to decide cases as they deem best, free from executive influence.

PROBLEMS OF REGULATORY ADMINISTRATION

The performance of the independent regulatory commissions has been seriously criticized. Six major criticisms have been leveled against them.

DECISIONS ARE DELAYED Months and years are required to obtain decisions in many cases. There are several reasons: First, by and large, the commissions simply have not had adequate budgets or staffs to handle the steadily increasing volume of work; secondly, in some commissions, particularly the FPC, new problems such as that posed by the regulation of natural gas sales produced an unmanageable number of cases to be decided; thirdly, delay has resulted in many cases because the commissions were simply unable to make up their minds on complex situations, e.g., the introduction of color television in the mid-forties.

Delay adds to costs, both for the commissions and for the companies or individuals regulated. In creating commissions to handle cases formerly decided by the courts, Congress expected that utilizing expert staffs, and following more informal procedures than the courts use, the commissions could decide cases promptly. These expectations have not been realized.

Many hearings extend over months, produce tens of thousands of pages of "record" to be analyzed, and require the employment of large legal staffs at large costs for the regulated companies. In many instances the large cost is a consequence of dilatory and overly legalistic practices of lawyers before the commissions; desiring to make every effort to protect their clients, they insist upon presenting all conceivably helpful evidence and use every maneuver. The objective of prompt and economical decisions has not been achieved.[5]

ADMINISTRATIVE PROCEDURES HAVE NOT BEEN SIMPLIFIED The commissions have tended to "judicialize" their proceedings. This step has been gradually taken to ensure that the airlines, security exchanges, or employers whose interests are the subject of policy making, prosecution, or adjudication shall be given every protection of "due process" in administrative and quasi-judicial proceedings designed to make use of the expert analyses of engineers, accountants, and others.

A long succession of court decisions and finally enactment of the Administrative Procedures Act in 1946 have established procedures to protect the rights of the parties. The decisions and this legislation have assured fair dealing but not expeditious or economical procedures. They have, in the name of "due process," discouraged the adoption of shortcuts or the modification of procedures to put experts to work on each problem and bring about more prompt and economical decisions.

A further criticism of prevailing procedures is that the commissions have not clearly distinguished between what they need regulate and what decisions should be left to the managements of the companies they regulate. For example, few are likely to question the necessity of regulating airline charges. But there is much controversy as to whether the CAB does not reach too far when it determines whether the airlines should or should not experiment with new lower coach fares, or with airline shuttle service.

POLICIES AND PLANS HAVE NOT BEEN DEVELOPED The statutes creating these commissions (with the exception of the NLRB) have in varying degrees of specificity placed on them the responsibility for establishing national policies. For example, legislation fixes on the ICC responsibility for formulating policies to guide the development of the rail and truck transport industries.

[5] James M. Landis, *op. cit.*, pp. 5, 6, and 7, cites data from each of the commissions' records showing that delays of two or three years in individual cases are not uncommon.

Formulation of policies in many areas requires that the commissions collaborate with other Federal agencies. For example, in formulating policies to guide the development of the energy resources at least four Federal agencies have a part. The FPC controls hydroelectric power and natural gas; the Department of Interior exercises significant controls over the production and distribution of petroleum; the TVA is a major source of electric power; and the ICC markedly influences the distribution of sources of power by its control over transport rates. Yet these commissions (and others) have demonstrated little ability to lead or to collaborate with other agencies in *formulating* urgently needed policies.

The commissions establish policies in every major decision they make. The CAB in its decision in the Southern Transcontinental Route Case, for example, established certain policies as to the distribution of air routes among the airlines. The commissions, indeed, influence policies in the choice of cases on which they make decisions. But the commissions, by and large, have failed to look ahead, to establish staffs capable of foreseeing problems, planning the actions needed, and weighing and promulgating policies to guide regulated firms in their meeting of such problems. In short, the commissions, the critics argue, have acted too much like courts making policies only as they decide each successive case, rather than acting like administrative agencies responsible for formulating national policies to guide their own decisions and to influence the actions of regulated industries.

ORGANIZATION IS INADEQUATE The commissions have seldom organized staffs capable of studying a broad problem of an industry (e.g., the need for regulation of the variable annuity insurance companies) and recommending policies in advance of the necessity of deciding cases. Hence, some propose that the policy functions of these commissions be transferred to executive departments (e.g., transportation policy to Commerce) and separated from the adjudicatory function (e.g., decisions as to rail freight rates by the ICC).

The commissions have lacked authority to organize effectively to handle the great volume of decisions they turn out. The central question is: How much authority to decide cases can they delegate to their staffs? The individual commissioners, or the commission as a body simply cannot personally decide the volume of cases that come before each commission. However, the courts and the Congress (and many lawyers who serve on the commissions!) prevent or limit their delegation of large authority to their expert staffs to decide many of the more routine cases, or cases for which the commission has established clear policies to guide these staffs.

Finally the commissions are criticized as being "headless." The multimembered boards that control the commission have, over the years, been reluctant to give their chairmen or any single staff member adequate authority to manage the staff and see that the work of the commission moves along. To provide for leadership or management the chairmen of several commissions were given authority to manage administrative operations (e.g., preparing the budget, hiring, promoting, or firing employees, and the general direction of the staff). In some instances an executive director was established to carry out the chairman's directions. In the sixties the position of executive director has tended to disappear, but the authority of the chairman has been enlarged. Yet the problem remains, for a chairman finds little time to give to directing and evaluating the work of a staff of one thousand or more *and* participating in the numerous hearings and formal meetings of the commission.

RESPONSIBILITY TO THE PRESIDENT AND THE CONGRESS IS NOT CLEAR   The President has a clear responsibility for seeing that the laws enacted by the Congress are faithfully executed; e.g., if the Congress has legislated that a national plan for the development of a civil air transport system shall be established and carried out, the President is responsible for seeing that this is done. The President simultaneously has a responsibility to lead the American people in utilizing the powers of the Federal government to meet emerging problems, for example, providing mass transportation systems for suburban areas sprawling over three or more states, a problem which lies at the root of cases being dealt with by the ICC and several other executive agencies.

The President's power to influence the commissions is limited by the extent to which they have been made "independent." That independence, however, is limited by four presidential powers. First, he appoints members to each commission subject to the approval and confirmation of the Senate. Secondly, he recommends to Congress the budget for each commission. Third, the President reviews any major legislation recommended by the commissions to the Congress and can propose such legislation as he deems desirable. Fourth, the President has, in most instances, the right to designate a member of each commission to be chairman.

Yet, it is contended that the President should have greater influence over each commission's activities. This contention is founded on the belief that in a democracy the elected chief executive should be able to integrate the actions, i.e., the policies and case decisions, with other national policies for which the President stands.

The commissions carry out a quasi-legislative function in that they interpret and give concrete meaning to actions of the Congress when they formulate policies and make rules. Hence, some contend that the commissions have an especial responsibility to the Congress; in practice a number of the commissions, at times, have been the handmaidens of particular congressional committees. This limits their independence and makes them ineffective in carrying out the President's program.

MEN OF UNIFORMLY HIGH CALIBER AND INTEGRITY HAVE NOT BEEN AT-
TRACTED   Observers of the commissions contend that the general level of personnel appointed to serve as members of the commissions is not high. There are notable exceptions: Joseph Eastman, who once served as a member of the Interstate Commerce Commission; William O. Douglas, now a Supreme Court justice and once a member of the SEC; William McChesney Martin, Chairman of the Federal Reserve Board; and Wayne Coy, once Chairman of the Federal Communications Commission. Despite these exceptions the record clearly supports the contention of the critics. Moreover, there is a substantial turnover among the members of the commissions; a majority tend to serve less than the terms of five or seven years for which they are appointed. Many leave to take positions in the industries they once regulated or to practice before the commissions on which they served.

The commissions also have been criticized for the unethical conduct of their members. A member of the FCC was effectively removed in 1959 for having accepted payments from a representative of a television station seeking a franchise from the Commission. In other instances, members of the commissions have been criticized for accepting favors, i.e., transportation, honoraria, or "boat trips," from important members of the industry they regulated or from the associations of those industies. In still other instances, the commissions have been criticized for hearing, in ex parte discussions, the views of representatives of the industries.

The task of the commissions exposes its members to such criticisms. The cases they are called upon to decide involve large stakes, and powerful economic interests, e.g., the natural gas companies, the television networks. This impels the companies regulated (individually or in concert) to try to influence or to dominate the commissions.

Yet, if commission members are to acquire the knowledge that is required for efficient conduct of their responsibilities, they must have a first-hand acquaintanceship with the industries they regulate. They must know and visit with representatives of the industry to obtain such familiarity. But if they do associate frequently with representatives of the industry they may lose the confidence of the public in their impartiality.

SUMMARY

The regulatory commissions, at the time of their origins, were looked upon as a novel and ingenious response to emerging needs for public action on economic problems. While their continued existence and growth is clear proof that they are essential for effective government, their performance has been repeatedly criticized.

A number of instances of authoritative and efficient action counter such criticisms: to wit, the FRB and SEC have a general reputation as well-managed agencies; the FTC's basing point study and the CAB's study of international air routes demonstrated that these commissions can formulate considered policies to meet basic problems; and the FPC's aggressive attack on the natural gas rate problem in 1962 demonstrated its capacity to innovate methods to meet adjudicatory problems. Simultaneously, significant improvements have been made in the organizations of several commissions.

All this is well, for the prospect is that government will regulate more activities, not less, in the future. Consider a single example: The prospect of transporting freight, if not persons, as well as communicating in space forecasts the need for regulation in a new field.

In short, in a democratic, capitalistic society in which large private enterprises exist and grow beside large government, it is increasingly necessary that there be machinery for regulation of individual enterprises in the public interest. Much progress was made during the late fifties and early sixties in improving the organizations and management of the regulatory commissions. Much remains to be done if these agencies are to lead in planning for the effective and profitable utilization, for example, of competing railroads, truck lines, and airlines, or for the continuing scrutiny of the security exchanges, while maximizing the freedom of the individual enterprise.

Review Questions

1. How does competition control economic activity? In what industries or economic activities has competition been replaced by government controls?

2. What were the earliest forms of government regulation of economic activity?

3. What agencies exist to regulate transportation? Which is responsible for coordinating air, water, and land transportation?

4. What is meant by (*a*) regulation by law (*b*) "regulation by franchise"? Why has regulation by administrative agency replaced these alternative forms of regulation?

5. What kinds of competitive practices have been outlawed by statutes?

6. What trends in the American economy gave rise (*a*) to the regulation of investment, (*b*) to the regulation of labor relations?

7. What aspects of their work distinguish the regulatory commissions?

8. What is meant when it is said that the regulatory commissions are responsible for both prosecutory and adjudicatory functions?

9. In what ways have the organizations of the commissions been found inadequate?

10. To what extent are the the commissions responsible to (*a*) the President or (*b*) the Congress?

For Further Reading

AMERICAN ASSEMBLY: *The Federal Government Service: Its Character, Prestige and Problems*, American Assembly, Graduate School of Business, Columbia University, New York, 1954.

APPLEBY, PAUL: *Policy and Administration*, University of Alabama Press, University, Ala., 1949.

ARGYRIS, CHRIS: *Personality and Organization*, Harper & Row, Publishers, New York, 1957.

BERNSTEIN, MARVER H.: *The Job of the Federal Executive*, The Brookings Institution, Washington, D.C., 1958.

CHARLESWORTH, JAMES C.: *Government Administration*, Harper & Row, Publishers, New York, 1951.

CORSON, JOHN J.: *Executives for the Federal Service*, Columbia University Press, New York, 1952.

COUNCIL OF ECONOMIC ADVISERS: *The American Economy in 1961: Problems and Policies*, a Statement before the Joint Economic Committee of the U.S. Congress, Mar. 6, 1961.

DAVID, PAUL T., and ROSS POLLOCK: *Executives for Government*, The Brookings Institution, Washington, D.C., 1957.

GULICK, LUTHER and URWICK, L.: *Papers on the Science of Administration*, Institute of Public Administration, New York, 1938.

HAIRE, MASON (ed.): *Modern Organization Theory*, John Wiley & Sons, Inc., New York, 1959.

HUNTINGTON, SAMUEL P.: *The Common Defense: Strategic Programs in National Politics*, Columbia University Press, New York, 1961.

LANDIS, JAMES M.: *Report on Regulatory Agencies to the President-elect*, Printed for the use of the Committee on the Judiciary, U.S. Senate, Washington, 1960.

LEPAWSKY, ALBERT: *Administration: The Art and Science of Organization and Management*, Alfred A. Knopf, Inc., New York, 1949.

LIKERT, RENSIS: *New Patterns of Management*, McGraw-Hill Book Company, Inc., New York, 1961.

MARCH, JAMES G. and HERBERT A. SIMON: *Organizations*, John Wiley & Sons, Inc., New York, 1958.

MILLETT, JOHN D.: *Management in the Public Service*, McGraw-Hill Book Company, Inc., New York, 1954.

————: *Government and Public Administration*, McGraw-Hill Book Company, Inc., New York, 1959.

MORSTEIN, MARX F. (ed.): *Elements of Public Administration*, 2d ed., Prentice-Hall, Inc., Englewood Cliffs, N.J., 1959.

NEUSTADT, RICHARD E.: *Presidential Power*, John Wiley & Sons, Inc., New York, 1960.

NIGRO, FELIX: *Public Administration*, The Ronald Press Company, New York, 1953.

PFIFFNER, JOHN and R. VANCE PRESTHUS: *Public Administration*, 3d ed., Harper & Row, Publishers, 1957.

POWELL, NORMAN J.: *Personnel Administration in Government*, Prentice-Hall, Inc., Englewood Cliffs, N.J., 1956.

PRESTUS, ROBERT: *The Organizational Society*, Alfred A. Knopf, Inc., New York, 1962.

ROSSITER, CLINTON: *The American Presidency*, New American Library of World Literature, Inc., New York, 1956.

ROWAT, DONALD C.: *Basic Issues in Public Administration*, The Macmillan Company, New York, 1961.

SELZNICK, PHILIP: *Leadership in Administration*, Harper & Row, Publishers, New York, 1957.

SIMON, HERBERT A.: *Administrative Behavior*, 2d ed., The Macmillan Company, New York, 1957.

—— et al.: *Public Administration*, Alfred A. Knopf, New York, 1950.

STAHL, O. GLENN: *Public Personnel Administration*, 4th ed., Harper & Row, Publishers, Incorporated, New York, 1956.

TORPEY, WILLIAM G.: *Public Personnel Management*, D. Van Nostrand Company, Inc., Princeton, N.J., 1952.

WALDO, DWIGHT: *Issues and Ideas in Public Administration*, McGraw-Hill Book Company, Inc., New York, 1953.

WHITE, LEONARD D.: *Introduction to the Study of Public Administration*, 4th ed., The Macmillan Company, New York, 1955.

Index

Administration, public (see Public administration)
Administrative Procedures Act, 140, 142
Administrative processes, 15
Agencies (see Independent agencies)
Agency for International Development (AID), 13, 60, 91
Air Mail Act of 1925, 128
American Telephone and Telegraph Company, 130, 139
Antitrust Division of Department of Justice, 61, 131–132
Appleby, Paul, 10n.
Applied Physics Laboratory, 97
Appropriations committees, 119–121
Argyris, Chris, 21n., 29n.
Armed forces (table), 85
  mobilization and training of, 84, 86
  support of, 88–89
  utilization of, 89–90
  (See also Defense)
Armed Forces Policy Council, 80
Armed Services Committee, 93
Arms Control and Disarmament Agency, 88
Atomic Energy Commission, 24, 71, 79, 115
Atoms for Peace Program, 60
Attorney General, 61

B-70 aircraft dispute, 89, 117
Barnard, Chester I., 19n., 23n.
Beard, Charles A., 14
Boards, 24, 138
Budget, 112–118
  congressional committees on, 120
  receipts, 107
Budget and Accounting Act of 1921, 9, 53, 122
Bureau of the Budget, 53, 55, 113–116, 122
Bureau of Labor Statistics, 43
Bureau of Old Age and Survivors Insurance, 68, 112
Bureaucracy, 20
Bush, Vannevar, 6
Business compared with public administration, 12
  (See also Corporations)

Cabinet, 114
Career executives, 30

Career system defined, 39
Carrier regulation, 136
Central Intelligence Agency (CIA), 56, 78
Civil Aeronautics Act of 1938, 128
Civil Aeronautics Board (CAB), 128, 138, 143
Civil defense, 91–93
Civil service, 37
  defined, 39
  (See also Public service)
Civil Service Commission, 39, 41, 48, 50, 53, 57
Civil service examinations, 39, 44
Civilian control of defense, 96–97
Classification of positions, 42–43
Clayton Act of 1914, 131, 135
Cole v. Young, 49
Collective bargaining, 46, 135
Commission on Efficiency and Economy of 1910, 9
Commission on the Organization of the Executive Branch of the Government, 1949 and 1955, 9, 27
Commissions, use of, 24
Commodity Credit Corporation, 25
Communication, regulation of, 130
Communism and loyalty investigations, 47–49
Competition, regulation of, 131
Comptroller General, 36
Congress, appropriations, 114
  authorization, 119
  in budget making, 119–122
  committees, 72, 119
  delegation of regulatory powers, 137
  and Department of Defense, 89, 93–94
  hearings, 115, 120
  Joint Economic Committee, 110
  relations to departments and agencies, 72
Congressional Reorganization Act of 1946, 122
Consolidated appropriation, 122
Contracting out, 111
Corporations, under Department of Defense, 97–98
  government, 25
  government contracts with, 111–112
  (See also Private enterprise)

Corson, John J., 44*n*.
Council of Economic Advisers, 55, 101, 114
Council of State Governments, 9
Credit programs, 104–106

Debt, national, 108
Defense, 76–99
  budget reform in, 94
  civil, 91–93
  civilian control of, 96–97
  command lines, 82
  Department of (*see* Department of Defense)
  development of weapons, 86–88
  military assistance to other countries, 90–91
  military programs, budget, 95
  military support, 88–89
  mobilization and training, 84–86
  scientific research and development, 5–6
  strategic planning, 83–84
  utilization of forces, 89–90
Defense agencies, 82, 89
Department of Agriculture, 63–64, 132
Department of Commerce, 64–66, 128
Department of Defense, 59, 76–99, 115
  administrative process, 80–83
  and Department of State, 78–79
  military programs, budget, 95
  nonprofit corporations under, 97–98
  organization of, 81
  scope of, 76–77
Department of Health, Education, and Welfare, 68, 69, 109, 132
Department of the Interior, 66–67
Department of Justice, 61–62, 131
Department of Labor, 67–68, 136
Department of State, 59–60, 78–79
Department of the Treasury, 60–61, 106, 113
Departments, listed, 58–63
  relationship to Congress, 72–73
Director of Research and Engineering, 80, 86

Economy, government and, 100–124
Egger, Rowland, 73*n*.
Eisenhower, Dwight D., 49, 53
Employee organizations, 45
Employment in government, 36–39
Employment Act of 1946, 55
Etzioni, Amatai, 21*n*.

Examinations in public service, 39, 44
Executive departments (*see* Departments)
Executive Office of the President, 9, 53
Executives, career and political, 30
  in government, 30
  leadership function, 33–34
  roles of, 31
Expenditures, 108–112
  in budget, 116–117
  increase in, 2–3

Fair Labor Standards Act of 1938, 136
Fallout shelters, 92
Farm subsidies, 110
Federal Aviation Agency (FAA), 69, 80, 128
Federal Bureau of Investigation, 61
Federal Communications Commission (FCC), 131, 139, 145
Federal government (*see* Government)
Federal Power Commission (FPC), 130, 139, 143
Federal Reserve Banks, 102
Federal Reserve Board, 103
Federal Reserve System, 102
Federal Trade Commission (FTC), 132, 146
Finance and credit regulation, 137
Finance Committee (Senate), 119, 120
Financial administration, 16
First Hoover Commission, 9
  for integrated executive, 27
Food and Drug Administration (FDA), 132, 138
Foreign affairs, 7–8, 59–60
Forrestal, James, 13

Gaus, John M., 19*n*.
General Services Administration (GSA), 53, 58
Government, as employer, 36–39
  executives in, 30
  expenditures (*see* Expenditures)
  growth of, 2–3
  organization, 23–26, 29–34
  purchases, 111–112
  regulating private enterprise (*see* Private enterprise regulation)
  role in society, 2
  structure, 54
Government corporations, 25
Grants-in-aid, 109, 118
Gulick, Luther, 10*n*.

Harris, Joseph P., 73n.
Hatch Act, 40, 48
Hawthorne studies, 11, 22
Henry, Laurin, 53n.
Hoover Commission, First, 9, 27
  Second, 57n.
Housing and Home Finance Agency,
  70
Hull, Cordell, 59

Independent agencies, 69–70
  budget for, 114, 115
  for defense, 78-80, 82
  regulatory, 138–139
  responsibility to Congress, 72–73
  in science, 71–72
Informal organization, 23
Information Agency, U.S., 60
Interstate Commerce Commission
  (ICC), 127, 139, 142
Investment, regulation of, 133–135

Jackson, Andrew, 38
Joint Chiefs of Staff, 82–83
Joint Committee on the Economic
  Report, 119
Justification books, 115, 121

Kennedy, John F., 53, 56, 70, 74, 92,
  108, 123, 129

Labor, regulation of, 135–136
Labor-Management Relations Act of
  1947 (Taft-Hartley Act), 136
Labor unions in Federal service, 45
Landis, James M., report of, 126n,
  142n.
Leadership, presidential, 73
Legislative budget, 122
Likert, Rensis, 11n, 21n, 34n.
Loans, government, 103–106
Lobbies, 72, 93
Logistics Management Institute, 97
Loyalty investigations, 47–49
Loyalty requirements, 39–40
Lukens, Mathias E., 33n.

MAAGS, 90
Management, 29, 33
March, James G., 21n.
Merit system defined, 39
Metropolitan areas, 4–5, 46
Military forces (see Armed forces;
  Defense)

Military programs, in Defense De-
  partment, 95
  for other countries, 90–91
  (See also Defense)
Municipal Manpower Commission, 38
Municipal research bureaus, 8

National Aeronautics and Space Ad-
  ministration (NASA) 24, 32, 71,
  78, 115
National Aeronautics and Space
  Council, 79
National Defense Establishment, 94
National Labor Relations Board
  (NLRB), 135, 142
National Science Foundation, 6, 71
National Security Council (NSC),
  56, 78
National Security Resources Board,
  56
NATO (North Atlantic Treaty Or-
  ganization), 90
Nonprofit corporations, 97–98
Norris-LaGuardia Act of 1932, 135

Office of Civil and Defense Mobilization (OCDM), 92
Office of Emergency Planning
  (OEP), 56, 78
Office of Science and Technology, 6,
  72
Office of Scientific Research and Development, 6
Old Age and Survivors Insurance,
  112, 118
Organization, 17–35
  characteristics of, 19–21
  elements of, 18–19
  government, 23–26, 29–34
  informal, 23
  public administration model, 26–29
  study of, 21–22

Patronage appointments, 41
Performance-type budget, 120
Personnel administration, 38–49
  changes in, 41–42
  organization for, 42
  terms defined, 39
Pfiffner, John M., 21n.
Population, growth of, 3–6
Post Office Department, 63–63
Presidential leadership, 73–74
President's Committee on Adminis-
  trative Management of 1937, 9

President's staff, 52–58
Pressure groups, 72, 93
Presthus, Robert, 20*n*.
Pritchett, C. Herman, 62*n*.
Private enterprise regulation, 123, 125–146
 antitrust laws, 131–132
 investment, 133–135
 transportation, 127–129
 unfair competition, 132–133
 utilities, 129–131
Productive capacity, factors determining, 101
Public administration, characteristics of, 12–14
 definition of, 11–15
 organization model, 26–29
 study of, 8–11, 15–16
Public Contracts Division, 67, 136
Public debt, 108
Public enterprise, 25, 123
Public Health Service, 28
Public service, 9, 37–51
 classification of positions, 42–43
 control by bureaus and departments, 49–50
 defined, 39
 employee organizations and unions, 45–46
 examinations, 39, 44
 future of, 50–51
 promotion in, 45
 recruitment for, 44
 salaries in, 43–44
 training for, 45
 veterans' preference in, 47
Purchases, government, 111–112

RAND Corporation, 97
Regulation of business (*see* Private enterprise regulation)
Regulatory agencies, 126, 138
 report on, to President-elect, 126*n*., 142*n*.
Regulatory commissions, 136–146
Research Analysis Corporation, 97
Reston, James, 18
Robinson-Patman Act of 1936, 131
Roethlisberger, F. J., 23*n*.
Roosevelt, Franklin D., 53
Roosevelt, Theodore, 9

St. Lawrence Seaway Corporation, 25
Salaries in public service, 43–44
Sayre, Wallace S., 10*n*.

Science, agencies and departments in, 70–72
 government expenditures for, 5–6
Science Advisory Committee, 6
SEATO, 90
Second Hoover Commission, 1955, 57*n*.
Secretaries of departments, 59–69
Secretary of Defense, 78
 administration under, 80–83
 powers of, 94, 96
 public support of, 93–94
 tasks of, 83
Securities Exchange Act of 1934, 133
Securities and Exchange Commission, 133–135, 137, 146
Security Act of 1933, 133
Seidman, Harold, 25*n*.
Selznick, Philip, 22*n*.
Sherman Antitrust Act of 1890, 131, 135
Simon, Herbert A., 11, 29
Small Business Administration, 105
Smithsonian Institution, 5
Social security, 24, 112, 118
Social Security Act, 112
Southeast Asia Treaty Organization, 90
Southern Transcontinental Route Case, 143
Staff, in organization, 29
 President's personal, 53
 President's use of, 52–58
Steel price case, 123
Strikes by public employees, 46
Subsidies, 110–111
Supervision, types of, 34

Taft, William Howard, 9
Taft-Hartley Act, 136, 138
Tariff Commission, 60
Taxes, 106–108, 113
Technological change, 5, 7
Tennessee Valley Authority (TVA), 25, 70, 143
Thompson, Victor A., 21*n*.
Transportation, regulation of, 127–129
Truman, Harry S, 25, 48, 53, 136
Trust funds, 118

Unions, of public employees, 45–46
 regulation of, 135
Urbanization, increase in, 4
Utilities, regulation of, 129–131, 136

Veterans Administration, 28, 70, 112
Veterans' Preference Act, 40, 47

Wabash, St. Louis & Pacific R.R. v. Illinois, 127
Wage and Hour Division, 67, 136, 138
Wagner Act, 135
Waldo, Dwight, 11
Walsh-Healy Public Contracts Act of 1936, 136

Washington, George, 39
Ways and Means Committee (House), 119
Weapons development, 86
Weber, Max, 20
Welfare services, 112
Western Union Telegraph Co., 130
White, Leonard D., 10*n*.
White House Office, 53
Willoughby, W. F., 10*n*.
Wilson, Woodrow, 10, 12, 14